JN025774

キリストにおける
新たなまなざし

Seeing All Things New in Christ

川中 仁／編
Hitoshi Kawanaka, S.J.(ed.)

上智大学出版
Sophia University Press

モンセラート・グディオル：巡礼者 聖イグナチオ（1991年）
Montserrat Gudiol: St. Ignasi Pelegrí（1991）

目　次 / Contents

キリストにおける新たなまなざし

イグナチオ・デ・ロヨラの回心とその現代的意義

はじめに

　1521 年 5 月 20 日にパンプローナ要塞の攻防で重傷を負ったイグナチオ・デ・ロヨラ（1491-1556 年）は、故郷のロヨラ城での療養期とそれに続くマンレサでの滞在期に生涯の歩みの根本的な転換となるような霊的な体験をした。このイグナチオの回心 500 年を機に、イエズス会のアルトゥーロ・ソーサ総長は全世界のイエズス会に呼びかけ、2021 年 5 月 20 日〜2022 年 7 月 31 日を「イグナチオ年」（Ignatian Year 2021-2022）と定め、「キリストにおいてすべてのものを新たに見る」（"Ver nuevas todas las cosas en Cristo" / "To see all things new in Christ"）（自叙伝 30・2 番参照）という標語のもと、現代イエズス会のミッションを原点から再確認することになった。

　上智大学では、この「イグナチオ年」の呼びかけに呼応し、イグナチオの回心の出来事を振り返り、その現代的意義を探るべく、2021 年 10 月 9 日、イエズス会日本管区の全面的な協力のもと、上智大学神学部主催、上智大学キリスト教文化研究所とカトリック・イエズス会センターとの共催で、2021 年度ソフィアシンポジウム「キリストにおける新たなまなざし—イグナチオ・デ・ロヨラの回心とその現代的意義」"To See All Things New in Christ. The Conversion of Ignatius of Loyola（1521/1522）and its Significance in our Contemporary World" が開催された。

　シンポジウムでは、まず「イグナチオ・デ・ロヨラの変容」という題目で、ホセ・ガルシア・デ・カストロ・ヴァルデス（José García de Castro

Valdés）氏にご講演いただいた。ガルシア・デ・カストロ氏は、スペイン・マドリッドにあるコミリャス大学神学部の教授で、イグナチオ・デ・ロヨラ研究、またイエズス会の霊性の研究の分野では世界的な権威で、関連の多数の業績がある。ご講演ではイグナチオの回心の出来事が何よりも漸進的な変容のプロセスだったことを示されている。

　続いて、「イグナチオ・ロヨラの回心とそのサイコスピリチュアルな見方」という題目で、酒井陽介氏にご講演いただいた。酒井氏は、2021年9月でローマのグレゴリアン大学心理学科講師を退任され、現在は上智大学神学部および同実践宗教学研究科で教鞭をとられ、神学と心理学の協力と統合という視点で研究に取り組んでいる。ご講演ではキリスト教の霊性と心理学を統合したサイコスピリチュアルという切り口でイグナチオ・デ・ロヨラの回心に迫られている。

　シンポジウムのいわば主人公であるイグナチオ・デ・ロヨラとともに、イグナチオの回心の出来事において欠かすことのできない最も重要かつ決定的なファクターは、イグナチオの生涯に根本的な変容をもたらした超越的人格的他者としての「神」ということである。イグナチオの回心とは、まさにこの「神」とイグナチオとの間に起きた出来事だった。このような超越的人格的他者としての「神」の存在、またその「神」によってある人の生涯が変えられてゆくということは、あまりなじみのある内容ではないかもしれない。だが、超越的人格的他者としての「神」の存在とその働きについては、イグナチオの回心に続く、500年にわたる無数の人びとの生涯が、そのリアリティーを雄弁に物語っているのである。

　本書は当シンポジウムの講演をまとめたもので、ガルシア・デ・カストロ氏のご講演はオリジナルのスペイン語テキストと日英両言語の翻訳、また酒井氏のご講演はオリジナルの日本語テキストと英語の翻訳を収録している。なお、本書の英訳は、ガルシア・デ・カストロ氏のご講演の英訳を除き、すべて上智大学名誉教授シリル・ベリヤト氏による。

イグナチオ・デ・ロヨラとは誰か?

● 川中　仁

　イグナチオ・デ・ロヨラ（Ignacio de Loyola, 1491-1556）――誕生名：イニゴ・ロペス・デ・ロヨラ（Íñigo López de Loyola）――は、1491 年にカスティーリャ王国のギプスコア（現在のスペイン・バスク地方）の地方貴族の家に生まれた。イグナチオは、有力貴族の宮廷小姓としての出仕を振り出しとして、騎士としての修養を積みながら、華やかな宮廷生活を送っていた。『自叙伝』[1] の冒頭で、イグナチオは、その当時を振り返って簡潔にこう述べている。「彼は 26 歳のときまで世俗の虚栄におぼれていた。特に、むなしい大きな名誉欲をいだき、武芸に喜びを見いだしていた。」（自叙伝 1・1 番）

　1521 年 5 月、イグナチオの生涯の最大の転機となるような出来事が起こる。スペインとフランスとの間に戦争が勃発し、イグナチオは、対フランス軍の前線基地であるパンプローナ城塞のスペイン軍守備隊の指揮を任された。攻め寄せるフランス軍の大軍に包囲される中、パンプローナ城塞のスペイン軍守備隊は頑強に戦った。だが、1521 年 5 月 20 日にフランス軍の一発の砲弾がイグナチオの足に命中し、重傷を負って倒れると（自叙伝 1・5 番）、スペイン軍守備隊はフランス軍に降伏した。敵方のフランス軍は、最後まで果敢に戦ったイグナチオに敬意を表し、

1　*El peregrino. Autobiografía de San Ignacio de Loyola*, Introducción, notas y comentario por Josep M.ª Rambla Blanch, S.I., Bilbao-Santander: Mensajero-Sal Terrae, 1998 (3ª Edición). 邦訳：聖イグナチオ・デ・ロヨラ『ロヨラの聖イグナチオ自叙伝』アントニオ・エバンヘリスタ訳／李聖一編、ドン・ボスコ社、2021年。

彼を騎士としての礼をもって遇し、故郷のロヨラ城まで送り届けさせた。ロヨラに到着したイグナチオは、負傷した足の治療のため、数回にわたり麻酔なしの過酷な手術を受けた。だが、その効もなく手術は失敗に終わり、結局彼の片足は短くなってしまった。イグナチオは、パンプローナ城塞の攻防で騎士としての栄誉を賭けて勇敢に戦ったが、たった一発の銃弾によって、将来の騎士として夢見て思い描き着々と築き上げてきたもの、そのすべてが一瞬のうちに潰えてしまったのである。

　イグナチオは、生家のロヨラ城で療養生活を送っていたが、何もすることなく暇を持て余していたので、ロヨラ城にあった2冊の書物を読むことにした。それはイエス・キリストの生涯を描いたキリスト伝——ルドルフ・フォン・ザクセンによる『キリスト伝（*Vita Christi*）』——とキリスト教の聖人たちの生涯を描いた聖人伝——ヤコポ・ダ・ボラジネによる『黄金伝説』（*Legenda aurea*）[2]——だった。イグナチオは、他に読む書物も無かったために、この2冊の書物を手に取って読み始めた。読み進めてゆくうちに、彼は次第にそこに描かれたキリストや聖人たちの生き方に心惹かれるようになり、やがて自分もキリストや聖人たちのような生き方をしてみたいと思うようになった。それは、キリストのように他者への奉仕に生きること、他者のために自らの生涯を捧げるという生き方である。こうして、騎士としての栄達を追い求めながら、騎士としての輝かしい未来のすべてを失ってしまった若きイグナチオは、全く新たな生きる意味と目的を見いだしたのだった。それは、これまでのように世俗の主君に仕えることではなく、新たな主君としてキリストに仕えるという理想であり、他者に仕えることを通して、キリストに仕えるという生き方である（自叙伝17・3番）。

　キリストの生涯に強く憧れ、キリストのように生きたいと思ったイグナチオがまず計画したのは、キリスト自身が生涯を送ったエルサレムに渡航し、キリストの足跡を辿ることだった（自叙伝45・3番）。こうして、

2　ヤコブス・デ・ウオラギネ『黄金伝説1〜4』前田敬作・山中知子訳、平凡社、2008年。

イグナチオは、故郷のロヨラを出発し、海路でエルサレムに渡航するために、バルセロナに向かった。だが、バルセロナへの途上にある小さな町マンレサに予定外の長期滞在をすることになった。イグナチオは、ここで自分を徹底的に見つめ直すとともに、彼の生涯を決定的に方向づけるような霊的な体験をすることになる。そのイグナチオ自身の霊的体験にもとづき他者のために役立つように祈りの方法をまとめたのが『霊操』(*Ejercicios Espirituales*)[3] である（自叙伝99・2番参照）。

　さて、1523年9月、イグナチオは、幾多の困難を乗り越え、ようやく憧れの地エルサレムに辿り着くことができたが、エルサレムを管理していた教会当局者はイグナチオのエルサレム滞在を認めず、イグナチオは再びヨーロッパに戻ることを余儀なくされた。こうしてヨーロッパに戻ったイグナチオがまず取り組んだのは、勉学だった（自叙伝50・3番）。それは、真に他者に奉仕するためには、自分には勉学と知識が決定的に不足していることを痛感していたからだった。

　イグナチオは勉学に取り組むことになったものの、それまで騎士としての修養しか積んでこなかった。そのため、勉学に取り組むにあたって、まず当時の学問研究に必須だったラテン語を修得しなければならなかった。イグナチオは、遥かに年若い学童たちと机を並べてラテン語学習に励むことから始めたのである。その後、イグナチオは、バルセロナを皮切りに、アルカラ、サラマンカなどのスペイン各地で勉学を続けたが、各地で教会当局者から嫌疑をかけられ、1528年、イグナチオは、当時のヨーロッパの学問研究の中心だったパリに赴き、パリ大学で勉学に取り組むことになった。その間、イグナチオは、キリストへの奉仕と他者への奉仕という、彼の理想と目的を共有する同志たちを獲得するための努力を続けていた。彼のそれまでの同志獲得の努力は、幾度となく手痛い失敗と挫折を繰り返していたが、パリでの勉学期間に、将来のイエズ

3　Ignacio de Loyola, *Ejercicios Espirituales*, Introducción, texto, notas y vocabulario por Cándido de Dalmases SJ, Santander: Sal Terrae, 2021 (8.ª edición). 邦訳：イグナチオ・デ・ロヨラ『霊操』川中仁訳・解説、教文館、2023年。

ス会の創立メンバーとなる同志たちと出会うことになる。

　パリ大学での勉学期間中に、パリ大学の学寮の聖バルバラ学院でイグナチオと同室となったのがフランシスコ・ザビエル（Francisco Xavier, 1506-1552）だった。ナバラ王国の貴族の家柄の出身で、陸上競技に熱心で、誇り高く野心に満ちた魅力的な若者だったザビエルは、当初、学寮で同室になったイグナチオに対する蔑みと嫌悪の念を隠さなかった。それは、眼前のみすぼらしい中年学生が、ザビエルの目指していたもののまさに対極となるものを体現していたからだった。それどころか、彼はイグナチオに対して敵意さえ抱いていた。その背景にあったのは、イグナチオが人生の決定的な転機を迎えることになった、あのスペインとフランスとの間の戦争だった。ザビエル家の当主は、ナバラ王国に仕える家臣であったが、ナバラ王国がフランス側についたため、スペイン軍と戦うことになった。フランスの敗北にともない、ザビエル家の居城であるザビエル城は、家族のための僅かな居住部分を残して、スペイン軍によって徹底的に破壊され、ザビエル家は没落することになった。ザビエルは、そんな非情な過去を背負いながら、キャリアアップを目指してパリ大学に留学していたのである。ザビエルは当初はイグナチオに激しく反発していたものの、イグナチオと接しているうちに、次第に彼の人柄や生き方に深く感銘を受け、徐々にイグナチオの目指す目的と理想に共鳴するようになり、遂にはイグナチオの最も信頼する同志の一人となったのである。

　こうして、1534 年 8 月 15 日、イグナチオを含む、最初の 7 人の同志たちは、パリのモンマルトルのとある聖堂で、清貧と貞潔とエルサレムへの渡航を主な内容とする誓願を立てた。このモンマルトルの誓願を立てた同志たちが、将来創立されることになるイエズス会という修道会の礎となったのである。このモンマルトルの誓願には、もし何らかの事情で 1 年間の待機期間を経てもエルサレム渡航の望みがかなわなかったならば、ローマ教皇のもとに赴き、ローマ教皇の指示を仰ぐという内容の付帯条項が付け加えられていた（自叙伝85・2-5 番参照）。イグナチ

オと同志たちは、1534年3月に「マジステル（magister）」の資格を既に取得していたが、1535年にはパリ大学での7年間にわたる勉学を終了し、パリを出発した。彼らは、イタリアでエルサレム渡航の準備をしていたが、その間にベネチアとトルコとの紛争が勃発したために、彼らのエルサレム渡航の夢の実現は絶望的となった。結局、イグナチオと同志たちは、エルサレム渡航の計画を断念し、ローマに赴いて教皇に謁見することになった。その後、1540年9月27日に教皇パウロ三世の教皇勅書「レギミニ・ミリタンティス・エクレジエ」（*Regimini militantis Ecclesiae*）によって、イエズス会は創立されたのである。1540年の創立以降、イエズス会は、瞬く間に急速な発展を遂げ、ヨーロッパ全土に活動の拠点を展開していった。イエズス会は、教育事業を修道会の活動の中心にすえ、もっぱら教育活動を通してイグナチオと同志たちの抱いた目的と理想の実現を目指して創立され、21世紀の現在にまで至るのである。

　イグナチオ・デ・ロヨラは、しばしばマルティン・ルターと比較され、宗教改革に対抗する反宗教改革の旗手のようにみなされている。だが、イグナチオという人物の生涯の歩みにおいて、少なくともその出発点となる「回心」には、対抗宗教改革的な意図は全く見えてこない。むしろ、イグナチオという人物の生涯を辿るなかで明確に浮かび上がってくるのは、キリストに従うということ、特に貧しいキリスト、遂には十字架につけられたキリストにまで従うということである。イグナチオにとって、キリストに従うとは、まず「キリストのように（*como* Cristo）」（霊操93・2番参照）、つまりキリストの生き方を模範とし、キリストのように生きるということである。
　貧しいキリストに従うという根本姿勢の基盤にはあるのは、聖書的信仰にもとづく神と人間の関係であり、圧倒的な神の働きによって人間との間に成立する関係である。ただ、その両者の関係は人間がただ無為のまま神の働きにまかせるということではない。聖書的な信仰にもとづい

て神と人間との間に成立するのは、神の圧倒的な働きとそれに応答する人間との間に成立する双方向の関係性である。このような聖書的な神と人間の関係について、新約聖書のガラテヤの信徒への手紙2章20節では、こう述べられている。「生きているのは、もはや私ではありません。キリストが私の内に生きておられるのです。」このパウロの言葉は、ややもすると純粋な他力のような印象をあたえる。だが、聖書の信仰によれば、人間は決して神によってプログラミングされたロボットのような存在ではない。人間は、一人ひとりにあたえられた自由意志において、キリストの圧倒的な働きに応えようとすることで神と人間との間に関係が成立する。このような神の圧倒的な働きにおいて成立する神と人間との間の双方向の関係を、イグナチオは、「キリストとともに（*con Cristo*）」――「わたしと共に（comigo）」（霊操93・3-4番、95・5番）――と表現している。このような超越的人格的他者としての聖書的な神の存在、そしてその神の圧倒的な力への応答ということこそが、イグナチオという人物の本質について理解する鍵である。

　ヨハネ福音書3章16-17節には、イエス・キリストの出来事全体の意義と目的が簡潔に述べられている。「神は、その独り子をお与えになったほどに、世を愛された。御子を信じる者が一人も滅びないで、永遠の命を得るためである。神が御子を世に遣わされたのは、世を裁くためではなく、御子によって世が救われるためである。」イエス・キリストの出来事とは、ただひたすら人びとの救いのためで、人びとのためにということにすべてが向けられていたということである。それゆえ、キリストのミッションとは、端的に人びとを助けるということであり、一人ひとりの人がかけがえのない存在として大事にされるような世界の構築である。そして、それこそがキリストの救いのわざを継続する教会のミッションである。

　イグナチオは、より良い世界の構築というキリストのミッションを救霊――「霊魂を助ける（ayudar a las ánimas）」――と表現している。ここで、イグナチオのいう「霊魂（ánima）」とは、人間の身体に対置され

た部分としての霊魂ではなく、むしろ人間全体を意味する概念である。したがって、イグナチオのいう救霊——「霊魂を助ける」——とは、人びとを助けることであり、人びとのために、ひいてはより良い世界の構築のために尽力するということである。自叙伝によると、イグナチオは、回心直後の早い段階からこの救霊ということを意識していたことがうかがわれ、例えば自叙伝45・3番には、回心直後のイグナチオについてこう述べられている。「彼の固くいだいていた決心は、エルサレムに永住して、たびたび、聖なる地を歴訪することだった。この信心のほかに、多くの人々の霊魂を救うことも決心していた。」このように、イグナチオにとって、キリストに従うということには、個人の生き方の選択にとどまらず、より良い世界の構築ということが明確に含まれている。

　より良い世界の構築というイエス・キリストの出来事にもとづくこのキリストのミッションは、すべての人びとと共有することのできる人類普遍の課題である。人類普遍の課題であるゆえに、宗教、信条などのあらゆる境界を乗り越えて、すべての人びとと手を携えて取り組むことができるのである。第二バチカン公会議を経て、現代のローマ・カトリック教会は、このキリストのミッションが、決してキリスト教以外の宗教に対してキリスト教の優位性を誇り、全世界にキリスト教の勢力を拡大しようとすることではないということを確認した。ただひたすら貧しいキリストに従うという望みに動かされたイグナチオの姿に迫るときにはじめて、イグナチオ、そしてイグナチオを師父と仰ぐイエズス会員たちの真の顔を知ることができるであろう。この望みこそ、イグナチオとイグナチオの遺志を受け継いだ後継者たちのミッションにほかならないのである。

イグナチオ・デ・ロヨラの変容

● ホセ・ガルシア・デ・カストロ

0 導入

　ロヨラ（スペイン・アスペイティア）のサンタ・カサ［イグナチオの生家］の三階には、「回心の聖堂」として知られる場所がある。その恐らくは30平方メートルの部屋はイグナチオの居室だったと考えられているが、パンプローナで負傷（1521年5月）して到着してから、夢と理想に胸ふくらませてエルサレムへと旅立つまで（1522年2月末）、9か月間の大半をそこで過ごした。

　この聖堂の天井の中心部分に記されている一節があり、こう述べられている。「ここでイニゴ・デ・ロヨラは自らを神に委ねた。」イエズス会の伝統では、イグナチオの「回心」の体験は、その療養期に体験し、主として信心深い読書（『キリストの生涯』と『聖人の華』）で動かされた内的なプロセスとそれが引き起こした霊の動きは同じものとみなされてきた。

　比較的短期間に、その望み、計画、価値、より深い感覚の領域の中でのあのように大きな変容がもたらされるためには、何か非常に深いものがイグナチオの内面で起こったはずである。ここで思い起こしたいのは、イニゴは1521年には成熟した人間であり（恐らくは30歳）、堅固な性格、今日では最早それが誰かは不明だが、ある宮廷女性を深く愛していたということである。

1 回心か変容／変貌か？

「回心」は、ロヨラでのイニゴ・ロペスの内面に起きたことをある程度まで的確に語るために、イグナチオ的な伝統で伝えられてきた言葉である。では、その9か月にわたしたちの主人公の内面に何が起きたのだろうか？

1.1 イグナチオの著作とイグナチオ・デ・ロヨラの初期の『生涯』における「回心」

最初のスペイン語の辞書（Covarrubias、1611年[1]）では、「回心」は、自然な生に固有の要素とされ、「ある存在から別の存在に変わること」、また「マグダラの回心のような罪人からの回心」（Cov. s.v. Convertir[2]）。「生涯の変化をも意味している。通常は悪から善への」、そしてアビラのテレジアの『生涯』第9章の用例が挙げられ、こう述べられている。「わたしには栄えあるマグダラへの篤い信心があり、しばしば、とりわけ聖体拝領時にその回心について思いめぐらした。」

イグナチオにおいて生じた明らかで確かな変化が認められるにしても、「回心」という言葉がイグナチオ的な用語法にはみられないというのは、興味深いがやや戸惑うことでもある。イグナチオは、この用語を生涯の変化には1度も用いていない（『自叙伝』、『霊的日記』、『会憲』、『霊操』にはみられない[3]）。『霊操』では、「キリストの生涯の秘義」の部分で一箇所登場し、霊操者が真の回心、「マリア・マグダラの回心」を観想するように招いている[4]。第一週では言及されず、そこで望ましいのは霊操者の「回

1　SEBASTIÁN DE COVARRUBIAS, *Tesoro de la lengua castellana o española*, Altafulla, Barcelona, s.v. Convertir.

2　著者は「つららや氷に変化する際の水」を用例として挙げている。

3　I. ECHARTE (ed.), *Concordancia ignaciana*, Mensajero-Sal Terrae-Institute of Jesuit Sources, Bilbao-Santander-St. Louis 1996.

4　「マグダラの女性の回心について聖ルカは記している。」（霊操282番）この秘義の説明につき、以下を参照。F. RAMÍREZ, *El Evangelio según san Ignacio. La* Vida de Cristo *en los* Ejercicios Espirituales *y la tradición bíblica en la* Vita Christi *del Cartujano*, Mensajero-Sal Terrae-U.P. Comillas, Bilbao-Santander-Madrid 2021, 537-559.

心」を呼び起こすことだが、それはイグナチオ的なポイントではない。

さらに驚かされるのは、イグナチオ・デ・ロヨラの生涯のこの時期について述べるのに、初期のいかなる伝記も公式文書でこの用語を用いていないということである。

初期の伝記の一つであるディエゴ・ライネスの伝記（1547年7月のボローニャからポランコ宛の長い書簡）では、イグナチオが療養期に悩まされた様々な霊の動きのプロセスに触れてから、ロヨラのこの時期を以下のように締めくくっている。

　　「誰も教えてくれる人もなく、誰にもその決意を伝えず、ナヘラ公爵の宮殿に行くという口実で、家を出て、故郷、所有物、自らの肉体をも**完全に捨てて、苦行の生活に入ることを決意した**」（『書簡』、4）[5]

ライネスは、ホアン・アルフォンソ・デ・ポランコのように、「回心」という言葉を避けているようである。彼は、1548年の『概要』の1年後、このライネスの言葉（『概要』、11）を字句通り繰り返している。だが、25年後に『イグナチオ・デ・ロヨラの生涯』（1575年）では、こう述べている。

　　「生活を変え、神にすべてを委ねることを（誰にも表明することなく）堅く**決意し**、考えて実際に行うことを**決めた**。すなわち、エルサレムに赴く。さらに肉体の苦行、名誉の放棄、つまり全面的な謙遜と厳格さで。神に大いに喜ばれることを望み、愛によるこの方法で**取り組む**ことを思いついた。他のより良いものはないと考えたからである。」（『生涯』、9）[6]

5　A. ALBURQUERQUE (ed.), *Diego Laínez. Primer biógrafo de san Ignacio*, Mensajero-Sal Terrae, Bilbao-Santander 2005, 136.

6　J. A. DE POLANCO, *Vida de Ignacio de Loyola* (E. Alonso Romo, ed.), Mensajero-Sal Terrae-U.P. Comillas, Bilbao-Santander-Madrid 2021, 56-57.

最後に、イエズス会の創立者に関する決定版とみなされている、ペドロ・デ・リバネデイラの『イグナチオ・デ・ロヨラの生涯』（1585年）は、イグナチオの過去の「秩序の乱れた」側面についてより詳細に述べているものの、そのスペイン語版には「回心」という言葉は含まれていない。

> 「学び［読書］に助けられながら、急いで前に進み［…］自己自身と**真剣に取り組み**、生活を**変え**、その考え方の舳先をそのときまでより確かで安全な他の港へと**まっすぐにし**」（『生涯』I, 2 [8]）[7]

これらの初期の四つのイグナチオ・デ・ロヨラに非常に近い著者たちの証言は、イグナチオの体験を描写する際に回心とは一定の距離をとっているように思われる。「決意した」、「自ら堅く決意した」、「真剣に取り組んだ」といった動詞から理解できるのは、回心について語るのにより望ましいかのように、イグナチオの内に起きた変化は、神の恵みの突然の介入というよりも、イグナチオの自由な意志の行為によるものだということである。

1.2　回心の聖書的な人物像

マグダラのマリアとタルソスのパウロは、中世後期の霊性の伝統で回心の事例とみなされてきた人物像である。すなわち、高みから受けた恵み、他者の顔、神のイニシアティブ、一定の突発性、生き方の突然の変化などである。

イグナチオに起こったことはそうではなかった。そのプロセスは、より緩慢で、瞑想的で、「わたし」の明らかな資質が神の恵みの静かな働きを確かめながら意識的に受け入れられたものだった。イグナチオにお

7　P. DE RIBADENEIRA, *Vida de Ignacio de Loyola, Fontes Narrativi IV*, IHSI, Roma 1965, 91. Moderna versión inglesa: *The Life of Ignatius of Loyola* (C. Pavur, trans.) Institute of Jesuit Sources, St. Louis 2014.

ける変容の内的なプロセスで起きた仕方は、同時代の霊的著作で理解される回心とは異なっていた。そこではその人物の生涯における神の突然で集中的な介入ということが強調される。その自由において、だが他方で聖霊からしめされたものに抵抗することも拒むこともできずに転換されるのである。ここで新約聖書の二つの人物像をみてみたい。

a. タルソスのパウロの回心

　イグナチオの精神性における回心、また初期イエズス会員たちと恐らくは同時代の霊性神学的な周辺環境の考えと体験は、霊操 175 番に描かれているような選定の第一の時機、多少とも自叙伝 8〜14 番でイグナチオに起きたことにより近いのである。

　実際に、霊操 175 番は、選定の第一の時機を描いており、ある人物がその生き方を転換する仕方が非常に簡潔に述べられている。それは、「罪」や王国の価値観に抗う状態にあって、そこからキリストに従う最初の段階から主にかかわる弟子や使徒までに、確実に、継続的に、疑いの余地なく転換するのである。イグナチオは、この霊操 175 番の最初の段落をパウロやマタイの召命から明らかにしている。だが、ロヨラで起こったことはそうではなかったのである。

　もし、「回心」ということが、ダマスコ途上のタルソスのサウロに起こったことと理解するならば、イグナチオに起こったことは「回心」と理解することはできないということは明らかである。というのは、イグナチオとパウロは、その原因（なぜ）でもその内容（なにを）でもその仕方（どのように）でも状況が異なっているからである。選定の第一の時機（霊操 175 番）は、同様の明白な契機において、神秘的な回心、召命、選定などの内容で一致する。それはその人格のうちに神が突然に介入して始まることによるもので、その人物の存在の内奥に到り、理解と理性（体験の解釈）、行為における自由さ（歴史的な決断）、そして明晰さ、確信、不可避的な確実さをもったすべてと意志／情動（体験）をつなぐのである。

b. マグダラのマリアの回心

　イグナチオの時代に「回心」ということで考えられていたことを理解するうえで、他の最も重要な聖書的な人物像は、マグダラのマリアである。イエスの聖テレジア（アビラのテレジア）は、次のような言葉で説明している。「わたしは栄えあるマグダラに信心があり、しばしば、とりわけ聖体拝領時にその回心について思いめぐらした。」（聖テレジア『生涯』第9章）コヴァルビアスの『宝典』は、回心の意味を説明するのに、この聖書の女性を含め、「マグダラのマリアの回心のような罪人の回心」と述べている[8]。イグナチオは、既にみたように、マグダラのマリアと回心の体験を直接に結びつけている（霊操282番）。それは恐らくは『キリストの生涯I』（60）：「マグダラの回心と悔悛」からとられたものである。だが、改めて、イグナチオに起こったことは、この福音書の箇所にみられるような、主との出会いではなかったのである。

1.3　イグナチオ・デ・ロヨラのプロセスの「再読」

　では、これらの初期の証言が回心について正確に語っていないのであれば、イグナチオ・デ・ロヨラには何が起こったのだろうか？　ロヨラでのイニゴ（1521～1522年）の内的なプロセスに「回心」という言葉を使うのを避け、その時代の著者たち（ライネス、カマラ、ポランコ、リバデネイラ）が語っているのは、そのとき起こったことは、その用語の通常の宗教的な意味での「回心」ではなく、徹底的にキリストに従うまでの一人の人物の内的な変容ということである。それは、疑い、闇、光、成功、誤りの中で展開していったもので、真正でキリスト教的な変容だが、疑いなく16世紀固有の守護聖人たちによる、通常かステレオタイプの道のりで推移したものではなかったのである。

　それでは、マグダラのマリアやタルソスのパウロにみられる回心とイグナチオ・デ・ロヨラに起こったこととはどこで区別されるのだろう

8　S. DE COVARRUBIAS, cit., s.v. *Convertir*.

か？　それは次の三つの点である。

a. その人物の歩む生活的かつ倫理的な状況。イグナチオは、キリスト
　者の迫害者（パウロ）か罪深い女性（マリア）というような、罪の
　倫理的な範囲には位置づけられない。
b. 神の恵みと主体の変容の関係がどのように起こったのかということ。
　つまり、マグダラのマリアやパウロにおけるような直接的で無媒介
　の神のイニシアティブによるものとイグナチオにおける主体の自由
　と決断の緊密な協働によるもの。
c. 回心か変容の体験に時間がどのように関係しているか。つまり、マ
　グダラのマリアとパウロにおけるように直接的だったかイグナチオ
　のように緩慢（9か月）であったか。

　では、ロヨラで起こったことはどうよぶべきだろうか？　それはある
状態Aから別の状態Bへという転換ではなく、ある人物の生涯におけ
る漸進的な転換である。それはその人の生活に徐々に表れ、ナザレのイ
エスを第一の強力な力強くひきつける中心とする新たな地平によって、
その情動、望み、計画において集中して引きつけられるのである[9]。
　聖霊の働きは、イグナチオの慰めと自由さの関与を通して、その意図
と決意を通して、後退することのない決断をつくりあげてゆくのである。
　どういうにせよ、思い起こさなければならないのは、ロヨラで起こっ
たことは「第一の、最初の、原初の」体験だったということで、それは
一方で1517年の26歳のイグナチオによって生きられたものそれ以前
の軌跡を特別の仕方で帯びており、他方でそれはその後の残された35
年間に生きることになるものを理解するための枠組みをあたえる[10]。
　だが、この体験は何に由来するのだろうか？　それはどこに存するの
だろうか？　その直近の未来のどこに向けられているのだろうか？　と

9　ガルシア・マテオは、変化について「カルトゥルジオ会士の『キリストの生涯』からのイニゴ
　のロヨラの大きな変化」と述べている。*Manresa*, 61（1989), 31-44.

いうのは、すべてがロヨラで始まったわけではなかったのである。

2 イグナチオ・デ・ロヨラの変容

2.1 第一段階 生活の深みと密度（アレヴァロ／ナヘラ 1517年）

　パンプローナの戦いが1521年に起こり、イグナチオが1491年に誕生したのならば、パンプローナで重傷を負った時点で、イグナチオは30歳だったと結論づけることができる。

　この世の虚しさ、武芸の鍛錬、名誉を得ようとする虚しい望みなどを理解する体験の後、それについては自叙伝の最初の数節に触れられているが、そこで述べられているのは4年前の1517年の体験と思われる。では、1517年、26歳だったとき、イグナチオの生涯に何が起きたのだろうか？　ホアン・ヴェラスケス・デ・クエリャールは、カスティリア王国の会計局長で、イグナチオの恩人かつ保護者だったが、アレヴァロの宮殿から追放され、彼とともにすべての使用人や支持者、今日風にいうと、そのチームとともにそのカスティリアの町を去らなければならなかった。

　アレヴァロからの追放はイグナチオにいつまでも痕跡を残した。イグナチオの堅固な人格に強く当たった最初の「砲弾」は、フランスの兵士からではなく、その生涯を考え直すカスティリアでの挫折によるものだった。ナヘラに向かって、イニゴは哲学的—形而上学的な性格についての

10　［ロヨラの］回心の聖堂に記されている文言のバスク語の翻訳者は、こう的確に表現している。すなわち、"Jainkoarenganatu zen"（「主へと向かう」）は、"norengan"（「誰かにおいて」）か"norengana"（「誰へと」）かの選択（この場合："Jainkoarengan"［主において］か"Jaikoarengana"［主へと］か）ではなく、動詞が用いられている。その動詞は全力で「向かう」という意味で、ある場所や考えではなく、神のペルソナへと向かうということである。この動詞では、ある方向に向かうという意味が、「とどまる」、あるいは集中していることという意味に先行する。それゆえ、「自らを委ねる」と「向けられている／集中されている」の間には明らかな相違がある。特に、巡礼者とその動きにおいてであり、また神が働くのは、第一の意味では（賜物の）受け手においてであるのに対して、第二の意味ではすべてのものを自らへと引き寄せる「磁力」においてなのである。

新たな理解を体験し、それによって恐らくは非常な時の流れ、現在の儚さと瞬間々々の密度によって、生涯の深い意味について問うことになった。

すべての宮廷生活の皮相的な環境、空疎でうわべだけの雰囲気に背をむけ、大人として責任をもって生き始めるために、その生き方を転換するように呼ばれているように感じていた。恐らくは、人生が遊びではなく、人生が「真剣な」何かであることに気づいていた[11]。それは、ちょうど一度だけ走る、一本だけの、唯一無二でかけがえのない列車のようだった。アレヴァロを去りながら、「わたしは生きている」というその単純で根源的な一節が何を意味しうるのかを真に理解しようとするならば、遅かれ早かれ生涯の秘義に入らねばならないということに気づかされる。

2.2 第二段階　ナザレのイエスの生涯と秘義（1521 年 5 月）

この第一の理解が基盤となり、イグナチオが、4 年後にロヨラで彼を待ち受けている、第二の理解を寛大さと開かれた態度で受け入れさせる。もしその第一の学びがリオハの地で（1517 年）人生の深みに入るのを助けたならば、この第二のものがその生涯そのものの「源泉」へと導いたのである。

もし初期イエズス会員たちの証言（ライネス 1547 年、ポランコ 1548 年、カマラ 1553 年、リバデネイラ 1585 年）を分析すると、イニゴが、その生きていた世界に関して、慰めと荒みの二つの心の動きを体験していたことが明らかになる[12]。その二つの動きの一つである「慰め」は最初に働き、すぐにそのプロセスを動かすようになる。一旦始まると、両者は同時に動き、二つの動きは、変わりつつ起こり、情動をその反対へと向かわせる。

11　イグナチオの最初の理解は、恐らくはこのハイメ・ヒル・デ・ビエドゥマの言葉を引用して詩的に表現できるであろう。「人生は真剣なものだ／このことは誰もずっとあとになって理解し始める／多くの若者たちのように、わたしも／人生を軽んじていた」
12　イグナチオがわずかな情報から生きることができたその変容について以下で詳細な分析を試みた。J. GARCÍA DE CASTRO VALDÉS, "El proceso de simplificación de Ignacio", *El Dios emergente*, Mensajero-Sal Terrae, Bilbao-Santander 2001, 220-240.

かくも単純で、初歩的で、本が読めるということに関して非常に「乏しい」ということも含め、最も基礎的なレベルの教養（読解力）と今日ではみなされるものが、イグナチオには想像すらできず、コントロールさえもできなかった、すべての心理的かつ霊的なプロセスの起爆剤となったのである。自叙伝には、こう述べられている。ロヨラ城には「彼（イグナチオ）が以前読んでいたような本は全然なかったので、一冊のキリスト伝とスペイン語で書かれた聖人伝とが与えられた。」（自叙伝5番）

　イグナチオの回心のこの最初の読書の重要性を評価しないわけにはいかない。イグナチオに影響をあたえた、義理の姉アラオスのマグダレナに対して感謝しても感謝しきれないことは、療養期の「時間を過ごすための」信心深い読み物をイグナチオに提供したことである。

　イエスとその弟子たちの歴史と逸話を物語っている、カルトゥルジオ会修道士ルドルフ・フォン・ザクセンの貴重なテキストが、その役割をはたしたのである。その言葉とイメージは、少しずつイグナチオを虜にした。イグナチオは読み（1）、何度も読んで、惹かれたところを読み（2）、それらの書物がとても気に入ると述べるまでになった（3）（自叙伝11番）。

　想像できるのは、イグナチオが、一章ずつ『キリストの生涯』の頁をめくりながら、論理的な流れを追うことにはあまりとらわれなかったということである。一旦それらの書物を閉じると、読むのを休み、イエスの歴史が、まずは想像力と夢想の中で（4）、それから夢と望みの中で新たな生命を獲得することとなった。イグナチオは、ガリラヤ、使徒たち、幸いの説教、パンと魚、ハンセン病者、盲人、ファリサイ派などについての「考察」に夢中になった。

　想像力を通して、イグナチオは、新しい世界、それはとても魅力的で未知で、内面に浮かび始め、また心理現象と感受性の経路を通して自由に思いめぐらすということを体験し始めたのである。だが、何よりも、最も根源的に新しく驚くべきことは、その内面に呼び覚まされた「感情的な反響」（5）だった。

イエスの歴史によって、彼は命で満たされ、想像をかき立て、恐らくかつては決して感じることのなかった「新たな喜び」がもたらされた。イエスのことを、そしてイエスとともにあることを想像することが、それ自体で命、また新たな命の原因となった。それは、宮廷生活で過去15年間にわたってみてきたものとは異なっており、後年彼はそれを「快楽」とか「歓喜」（自叙伝1、8番；霊操35番）を呼ぶことになる。その喜びは格別のものだった。

　その15年後の1536年に、ヴェネチアで、彼のかけがえのない書物である『霊操』の最後の手直しをすることになる。霊操329番では、こう述べられている。「神とその天使たちに固有なのは、その動きにおいて、真の嬉しさと霊的な喜びをあたえる」ことである。これは第二週の識別の第一の規定である。イグナチオは、聖ベルナルドの何かの説教、ホアン・カシアノの講話、あるいはイグナチオに大きな影響をあたえたジャン・ジェルソンの論考で学んだ理論について語っているのではない。そうではなく、イグナチオは自らの「体験」、神のみから由来する感情や動きについて語っているのである。神は、それらをあたえ、喜びを引き起こし、その現存の喜びを伝えるのである。そのようなものを体験したのは初めてだった。

　この回心はどこに位置づけるべきだろうか？　もしアレヴァロを後にする1517年の最初の体験が、哲学的、実存的、形而上学的な内容の回心だとするならば、ロヨラの体験は、その生涯の宗教的次元にまでゆっくりと、だが止むことなく降ってきたのである。その違いは何だろうか？　その違いは、「神はここにいる」という全生涯の意味の地平と原理と基礎としての高みと超越が出現したということにある。

　もし哲学的な回心において主体が真理自体とその固有の生命の前のみにあるならば、こう自らに問いかけさせるだろう。「より良い人間になるためには、何をし、何をすべきだろうか？」宗教的な回心は、わたしたちが自らにこう問いかけることへと招く。「主よ、あなたにより良く従う者となるために、またあなたにより近くあるために、わたしに何を

望まれますか？」

　イグナチオは、幼少期から伝統的なキリスト教的な宗教教育を受けてはいたが、今や「宗教」ということは別のことを意味するようになった。この体験は、ナザレのイエス、謙遜なイエス、主、友、仲間であるイエスを、人格的、体験的で、慰めのうちに発見することにある。イグナチオは、宗教の生き生きとした体験的な次元に深く入り始め、イエスとともにある喜びを「感じ、味わう」ことを始めたのである。

　だが、イグナチオの体験は、イエスに情動的に引かれ、魅されたままであることに満足しなかった。イグナチオは、新たな主人と計画への畏敬のままにとどまったのではなく、熱意と力強さをもって、キリストに倣い、キリストに従うことのダイナミズムの中へと入っていた。ただし、読書で出会った使徒たちと聖人たちを模倣するそれ以上の論拠や方法論はなかったのである。

　イグナチオは、バランスを欠き、分別のない仕方で自由を駆使することを決断した。「まだ分別に欠く状態だったが」（自叙伝14番）、すなわち「生き方を変え、すべてを神に委ねることを自分自身で強く決意した（誰にも表明していなかったが）。考えて、これを実際に行うことを決意した。」[13]（『生涯』、9部）それは、友人や家族の意見では、無分別で不懸命なやり方であった（自叙伝12番参照）。

　イニゴは、地元の小教区の司牧計画と積極的に協働しながら[14]、ロヨラとアスペイティアにとどまることもできたし、周辺の最も単純な人びとの霊的生活を励ましたり、16世紀のNGOかのように、最も必要とされた人びとのための支援と連帯のための小さな組織をつくったり、慈善行為に捧げることもできた。

　だが、彼はそうしなかった。イニゴは、生涯のこの時期にキリストのために何か偉大なことを行うべきだと解釈し、可能な限り最も偉大なこ

13　ポランコの言葉は、「わたしは、欲し、望みます。また、これは熟慮された決定です」という霊操98番の一節を思い起こさせる。
14　スコルソォのサンセバスチャン教区は、彼の父祖が管理し、出資していた。

とを見すえた。だが、それは、モンセラートではなく、サンチャゴデコンポステラやローマですらなく、第一の源泉で、そこからすべてが始まった「エルサレム」に赴こうと模索したのである。

　それゆえ、「イグナチオは何に回心したのか？」という問いは正確ではない。彼の生涯のこの時期には、より的確なのはこう問うことである。「イグナチオは誰に回心したのか？」何よりも、それはある人格的他者であるイエスへの回心だった。このイエスに引きつけられ、魅せられ、格別の親しさを感じたのである。それは全面的に透明な回心ではなく、疑いもなく、やや不純で、イグナチオ自身が信じていたものの終焉だった。だが、それは、後のすべてのプロセスを可能にし、一貫性、記憶、意味をあたえるような、第一の原初的で十分かつ必要な体験だった。

　この当初のイエスとの親しさは、そのときまで彼の世界を形成していたものに対して穏やかな距離をとらせるようになった。イエスに引かれるままにすることで、それにともなって自らの過去の生活に対して距離をとることになった。知らずに、イグナチオは、14世紀の英国の古典『不可知の雲』の匿名の著者が忘却の雲とよんだところに入っていった。「このような聖なる望みは、今までの考えをしだいに忘れさせてくれた。」（自叙伝10番）

　聖霊がその作業の大半を行ってきた。恐らくそれはより困難な作業だった。それは、イエスの近くにあることで湧き出る謙遜さの新たな生態系へと情動的に引き寄せられるために、空しい栄光の旗に引かれないようにすることである。

2.3　第三段落　「わたし」を再形成する（マンレサ1521年〜エルサレム1523年）

　ここで、生涯の真剣さへと回心し（1517年）、イエスとの親しさへと回心し、エルサレムに赴くことを決断したイグナチオをみてみたい。

　だが、もしロヨラの体験がすべてを達成したと主張するならば、無邪気で、軽率で、楽観的な過ちを犯すことになる。イグナチオは、タボル

山へと据えられたまなざしで、イツライツ（ロヨラの山）の眺望を失った。だが、その変容は、彼自身が考えていたほどには根源的でも全面的でもなかった。イグナチオが回心したと信じたことと実際に回心したものは、部分的には一致していたが、すべてに影響を及ぼすというのとはほど遠かった。

　キリストの姿へと変えられてゆくプロセスは、想像しうる以上に、長く、また苦しい作業だった。エルサレムを夢見て、服装や靴を変え、巡礼杖を購入したり、爪や髪の毛をのばし放題にしても、情動的─性的な世界を転換させることも含めて、地上的な価値観、願い、野望の内面世界にこり固まった人格を変容するのには十分ではなかった。イグナチオの「わたし」は、もう30歳になっており、心理的感情的な複雑な構造は、パンプローナの城塞を攻略するよりも困難だった。

　マンレサで過ごした11か月（1522年3月〜1523年2月）にあらゆる無秩序や誘惑の世界に直面したが、モンセラートのベネディクト会修道士（ホアン・チャノネス）が忍耐と思慮と懸命さで同伴することができた。

　どのようにイグナチオがわずか数週間で（エルサレム）巡礼の「英雄的な」企てを前にして、いかなる障害をも克服できるような楽観主義と力強い歓喜のうちにあったのが、貧しさと極度の惨めさ、無意味感、自殺への誘惑、そしてもし少しでも光を得られるならば、野良犬の後にもついてゆこうとするところまで屈辱的な状態になったことを確認することができることに注意したい。「主よ、どこに助けを見いだせるかをお示しください。もし小犬の後に従って小犬から助けをもらうのが必要であれば、それもいたします。」（自叙伝23番）

a. イエスの記憶、不変の岩

　なお注意すべきことは、イエスに心がとらえられたこの人物は、このように深刻な危機に陥りながらも、アスペイティアに戻ろうとしなかったということである。真夜中に、過去の記憶がまぶしく輝いていたであ

ろう。「なぜ故郷に戻らないのか？」そこでもイエスとの関わりのうち
に生きることができるような、静かでキリスト教的な家庭の記憶が強く
よみがえってきたころであろう。「なぜ戻らないのか？」

　誘惑は思慮分別と良い考えの装いをしていた。「イニゴ、ロヨラに戻
って、所有地を管理し、家族の仕事を果たせ。イニゴ、アスペイティア
に戻って、農民たちの状況を改善させ、必要とされる人びとのために働
け。アレヴァロでのしっかりとした養成はロヨラでも役に立つ。イニゴ、
戻れば、結婚できるし、アスペイティア、ビルバオかサンセバスチャン
のまじめで、魅力的な女性は良き妻に回心するはずだ。」多くの考え、
そのすべては良いもので、とても人間的で、宗教的にも健全だった。

　だが、イニゴは戻らなかった。そして、この戻らないということが、
ロヨラでの体験の深さを物語っている。なぜイグナチオはその企てを放
棄しなかったのか？

　恐らくそれはロヨラで感じた慰め、神のみからくる真の喜び（霊操
329番）を繰り返し信頼したからである。ロヨラの体験はイグナチオの
記憶を満たし、イグナチオはそこに繰り返し戻り、その過去のうちに現
在のための光、未来の意義を発見したのである[15]。ロヨラでのイグナチ
オのイエスの体験は、新しい生き方の礎となる岩だった。雨と嵐が来て
も、その家はもちこたえたのである。イグナチオは感覚の闇の試練と放
棄の試練を耐え忍んだのである。それは真実であり、まさに真理だった。

　イグナチオが戻らなかったのは、体験したことを信じたからであり、
そのうちに神の現存が認められる、自らの力を信じたからである。ロヨ
ラで感じた慰めのようなものは感じられなくても、神がそこまでついて
くるという信仰を信頼したのである。エゴと悪霊は彼を困難で、しかも
非常に困難な状況に追い込んだ。だが、イニゴの心理は、その攻撃をも
ちこたえた。

15　ここには第一週の第11則（霊操323番）が響いている。慰めの記憶は荒みの試練を乗り超える
　　力をあたえる。「そのときのために新たな力を得る」

b. 最も過酷で持続的な戦いである「わたし」

マイスター・エックハルトはこう述べている。「自己自身を忘却し、失うことより偉大な男らしさ、戦争、戦闘はない。」[16] イグナチオが今戦わなければならないのはその戦いであり、遅かれ早かれ主に従おうとするすべての者が直面するものである。恐らく最も過酷だったのは、自らの愛、自らの判断の回心だった。その回心は、その生涯を委ねることであり、そして何よりも自己自身を委ねることである。エルサレムに到達する方が、自己自身の内奥に到達するよりも遙かに容易だった。

b.1 貧しさを識別する

聖人たちの模範に従い、イニゴは、実際の物質的な貧しさの実践をまた信じて、没頭した。それは可視的で数値化できる客観的な貧しさだった。食べ物、飲み物、断食、服装、睡眠、徹夜、鞭打ち、苦行など、だがそれはそれ自体で客観的な徳と解釈されるもので、見せかけの聖性に到達するための偽装された障害ともなりえたのである。

袋を身にまとっていたが、粗くごわごわした布の下には何があったのか？ 貧しくボロボロのサンダルだが、恐らくは隠されている何が、その明らかな素足を支えていたのか？

時とともに、イグナチオは、その目に見える明らかな貧しさが識別されなければならないことにも気づいていた。この最初の貧しさは、「自分が」ということ、あるいは自己中心性の要素も含まれていた。それは、多くの聖人たちが行ったような禁欲と犠牲を体験するのに十分な、自己陶酔的なエゴを助長しうるようなものだった。

用心しなければ、自叙伝を引用すると、「まだ分別に欠く状態ではあった［…］内的なことを少しも考えていなかった。謙遜や愛徳や忍耐、またこれらの徳を調和させる賢慮がなんであり、またこれらの徳をはかることがどんなことかも知らなかった。」（自叙伝14番）また、用心し

16　M. Eckhart, *El fruto de la nada*, Siruela, Madrid, 2001, 150.

なければ、貧しさとの関係そのものが、勝利の履歴の中で征服と解釈されることになる。それはイエスとともに、イエスへと謙遜さをもって歩むというふうに見せかけているというのと実のところ大差なかった。

b.2 その望み、道、意図…神の道？

　イグナチオに関して、自叙伝にしばしばでてくるのは、次のような表現である。彼の道（自叙伝17番）、彼の習慣、彼の決意（17番）、彼の固い決意（45番）、彼の計画、彼の望んだ装い（18番）ということである。エルサレムでは、テキストに繰り返しでてくるのは、彼の固い決意（17番）、彼の意図（45番）、彼の良い意図（46番）、いかなる恐れにも揺るがない決意（45-46番）。

　テキストで繰り返される、この「彼の」ということは、著者によって熟慮して意識的に選ばれたもので、次のことをわたしたちが気づくのを助ける。それは、イグナチオが自らの意志と欲求によって大きく導かれていることであり、また神の意志へと慰めのうちに委ねることへと入ってゆく（この現在分詞は重要）ために、常にプロセスにおいて、道において、自らに打ち克ってゆくという常に未決定の課題へと導かれているということである。

　イグナチオはすべてにおいて神が彼に求めつつあることに応答しようと努めながら、後に霊操32番の有名な段落に記すものを区別することを細心に観察しつつ学んでいた。「自らのうちに三つの考えがあることを前提とする。すなわち、わたし自身のもので、わたしの単なる自由と欲求からでてくるものである。そして、他の二つは、外から来るもので、一つは善霊から来るもの、他は悪霊からのものである。」

　イグナチオの体験の分析から、イグナチオは、自らの望み、欲求、意志からきたものと神の望みと意志からきたものを区別することを学んでいた。

　それは、剥奪、明け渡し、より劇的にいうならば、わたし自身の死にまでへと向けられている学びである。それは日々十字架を担う学びであ

り、その十字架が保証するのは、たとえそれが非常に福音的であるか、良いか、実際にそうであるか、あるいはそのように見えるものであっても、わたしたちの望み、意図、計画のみを担わないということだけではなく、わたしたちにおける神の望み、意志、計画、行為を信仰をもって引き受けながら生きるということである。わたしたちの命はわたしたちが考えるほどわたしたちのものではなく、何よりも、そしてすべてに優って神の命、わたしたちにおける神の命である。

　わたしの、また「自己自身」のこの回心には終わりがなく、漸近的な性格の体験である。ちょうどわたしたちの主がペトロになされたように、わたしたちが開かれているのは、イエスがいかなる瞬間にもわたしたちに呼びかけ、「イニゴ、わたしを愛しているか？」（ヨハ21章）と愛についてわたしたちに繰り返し問いかけていることである。さらにまた重要なのは、キリストのためのわたし自身による敬虔な偉業とは、エゴ中心から離れ、自発的にかつ決然と愛にとどまることである。偉業であるか否か、それは第二義的である。

2.4　第四段階　教会への望みと意志（エルサレム1523年）（自叙伝45-48番）

　この第三の回心は、貧しさのより人間論的―神学的で本質的な次元で、1523年9月末の突然の予期しない新たな光を獲得した。フランシスコ会の管区長は、聖地の管理者で、もし取り決めた期限までにエルサレムを離れ、出発地に戻らなければ、破門するとイグナチオを脅した。それは、歴史的な逸話以上に、疑いもなく両者にとって不快で、イグナチオにとってはあたかも別の新たな砲撃を受け、またも新たな生き方の方向性を無効にされたかのような新たな衝撃であった。

　イグナチオは、エルサレムにとどまるという「固い決意」（自叙伝45, 46番）でそこに到達するのに困難な2年間を費やした。今、20日間の文化的―霊的な訪問の後に議論の可能性や対話なしに故郷に戻らなければなかったのである。

「神の意志」という表現が自叙伝に最初に（！）でてくるのが、ちょうどこのエルサレムでの新たな危機後であることを確認できるのは興味深い。自叙伝から引用すると、「エルサレムにとどまることが神のみ旨でないとわかった後」（自叙伝50番）。

　教会的な権威とともに、イグナチオの回心のプロセスに新たな変数が明白かつ力強く飛び込んでくる。これまでは宗教的な体験には、イグナチオとイエスという二人の主人公がいた。彼らは巡礼者の内面性／主観性、緊密で、親密で、情動的な関係において出会っていた。

　だが、イグナチオは、今や法的のみならず神学的—神秘的な権威の源泉である第三の要素の体験へと開かれることになる。だが、イグナチオはまだそのことを理解していない。1523年には、道を離れ、この歴史的な契機にフランシスコ会の管区長が指示したことに統合するために従うことで十分だった。当惑と新たな挫折のただ中で、「教会—従順—神の意志」という結びつきを受け入れたが、この三つの結びつきをもたらし、基礎づける神秘を内的に理解するのにはまだ時間がかかることになる。

　イグナチオが今まで唯一で十分な基準として信じてきたことは、内面の識別された動きが、自分がキリストに従うことに的を絞って、識別のプロセスで迫られた道を求めるより高い要請によって、測り直されることだった。

　「自分が」という堅実な性格は、神との関係を理解する新たな方法へと開かれ続けた。この場合は、後に「わたしたちの聖にして母である位階的教会」（霊操353番）と表現されることになるものに対してである。

　このエルサレムの危機は、以下のポイントにみる道のりに開かれている。聖霊は、かのコヘレトの言葉により回心の要素の分量を決める。「天の下では、すべてに時機があり／すべての出来事に時がある。」（コヘ3・1）

2.5 第五段階　他者へのまなざし、神の顔（バルセロナ 1523 年～ パリ 1534 年）

　1523 年 9 月 4 日にイグナチオはエルサレムに入り、23 日にはベネチアに戻るためにヤッファに向けて聖都を出発した。たった 20 日であれほどの希望と力を注いだ夢が潰えてしまった。エルサレムでいったい何が起きたのか？　また、イグナチオの回心についてのわたしたちの探究で、この短期間に何を見なければならないのか？

　エルサレムでのイグナチオの歩みについてあまり情報はない。自叙伝でまた驚かされるのは、聖地でのイグナチオの出来事に 4 段落だけあてていることである（自叙伝 45-48 番）。そのうち、最後の 3 つの段落が出発の際のトラブルを説明するのにあてられている。内面の体験についてイグナチオはほんのわずかしか語っていない。「各聖域を訪れるごとに、いつも同じ敬虔な念を感じた。」（自叙伝 45 番）[17]

　この第五の理解／回心により深く入るために、再びロヨラに遡らなければならない。また、一方で「彼の」決意、他方でイグナチオが神の意志か否かということには考え過ぎて立ち止まることなしに、当初から受け入れていたあのイニシアティブに接近しなければならない。

　生家を離れるにあたり、イニゴが確信していたのは、神が彼を孤独な企てへ、孤独のうちに生活を転換し、再開することへ、また彼が最近見いだしたばかりの、新たな主であるイエスとの排他的なかかわりへの召命を生きるということである。

　これまで述べてきたことからこう結論づけられる。できるようになるとすぐに、オニャーテの兄弟と別れ（自叙伝 12 番）、その後「連れて来た二人の従僕とも別れ」（13 番）、モンセラートへと向かった。「ただ一人らばに乗って」出発し（13 番）、その後バルセロナからベネチアに向かい、「数人の人たちが同伴したいと願ったが、[…] 一人で行こうと決

17　ポランコによってもう少し知ることができる。「前に考えていたものよりも、霊的な慰めの味わいと感覚で一杯に満たされ、それから強い確信をもって知り、そこにとどまることを決意した」（『生涯』82 [30]。聖地でのイグナチオの滞在について触れた唯一の段落）

めた」（35番）イグナチオ自身はその理由を説明しているようである。

　「自分は信・望・愛の三つの徳を得たいと望んでいる。もし自分に同伴
　者があったら、空腹のときにはその人に助けてもらえると思い、倒れれ
　ば、その人が手伝って起こしてくれると思うであろう。こんなふうでは
　その人を頼り、そのため、この人に愛着を感じる結果になるかもしれな
　い。しかし、そういう信頼とか、愛情とか、希望とかは、ただ神に対し
　てだけもちたい。［…］一人で乗船するのみならず、まったくなんの用
　意もせずに行きたいと思った。」（自叙伝35番）

　では、この孤独のうちに召命に応えるという望み、「彼の」望みは、
イグナチオの中でいったいいつまで持続していたのだろうか？　私見で
は、恐らくはエルサレムからの帰還の旅路で、生き方のこの側面を見直
したのであろう。イグナチオを知っていれば、恐らくはヤッファを出発
した10月3日からベネチアに到着した1524年1月中旬まで（3か月
ほど）、わたしたちの巡礼者は、聖地で見て、体験したすべてのことを
思い起こし、祈り、「内的に感じ、味わ」っていたのであろう。
　思い起こせば、イグナチオは、イエスと同じ場所を歩むということが
その弟子たちと同じ場所を歩むということだと理解していた。だが、イ
エスが稀にしか独りで旅をせず、それゆえイエスの友たちと弟子たちの
一員となるということは、ある共同体やグループを形成し始めるという
ことを意味するということを、イグナチオは理解したのである。
　イエスのことを考え、その友たちの一部であろうと望むことは、必ず
あるグループのメンバー、友たち、弟子たち、仲間たちのグループのメ
ンバーと認められることだった。たとえ主人との間に築いてきたもとも
とのパーソナルな関係を断念するということになったりはしないにせよ、
イエスに従うということの社会的次元、その団体的で組合的構造、その
教会的な性格を理解し始めたということである。
　イエスと共にあることの新たな仕方と様式を考え直し、理解したとき

は、恐らくは聖地での体験からだったであろう。恐らくは、より自己自身を中心とせず、むしろより部分として、従う者たちのグループ、「イエズス会」「イエスの小さきコンパニア」と呼ばれることになる小さな教会のグループの一部という従い方に位置づけし直されたように、イグナチオは感じたのであろう。

　それゆえ、たとえ短くとも、エルサレムの体験が、この側面を理解する手がかりであり、弟子であると理解し、理解されるイグナチオの仕方のその前後で変わった特徴だったのである。イグナチオは、仲間たちと出会わなければならなかったのである。再びバルセロナで（1524年）、良き友人だったイサベル・ロゼーの寛大さのおかげで、アルカラ大学の入学が認められるため、また「霊魂を助けるための」勉学を始めることができるためとして、必要なラテン語のレベルを獲得することができた。海のカテドラルの町［バルセロナ］の時期は、ある仲間たちのグループを強化するための最初の試みの発端ともなった。

　バルセロナ、アルカラ、サラマンカは、イニゴがカリスト・デ・サ、ディエゴ・デ・カセレス、ホアン・デ・アルテガ、ホアニコと呼ばれていたホアン・レイナルドらと体験したハプニングについて少なからぬ情報を提供している。彼らは一緒に大学生らしい出来事、霊操の最初の適用、異端審問の当局者との少し厄介なトラブルを体験した。彼らはいい友人たちでお互いに好きだったことは確かである。イグナチオは、カセレスと実に不便な状況のもとサラマンカの独房で共に過ごした。皆は一緒にパリでの生活の新たな段階の計画を立てた。だが、その夢は現実のものとはならなかった。「パリに行こうと決心したとき、自分がまずパリに渡り、一同がパリで学問を続けるすべがあるかどうかを確かめるから、それまで、皆はサラマンカで待機するようにとりきめた。」（自叙伝71番）

　知られていることのすべては、この最初の仲間たちのグループは前進することはなかったということである。イグナチオはセーヌの町から頻繁に手紙を書いたにもかかわらず（自叙伝80番）、誰もパリへと旅立た

なかった。「カリストはポルトガルの宮廷、そこからインディアスに行」き、そこで裕福になって帰国した。「カセレスは故郷のセゴビアに戻った。」アルテアガは、メキシコの司教に任命されたが、「奇妙な事故」で死んだ。

だが、イグナチオのグループへの回心は、別の不可逆点だった。他の仲間たちとキリストに従い続けることを望み、パリで少し探し求めた後、バルバラ学院でサボイ人とナバラ人、ピーエル・ファーブルとフランシスコ・デ・ハソ、つまりフランシスコ・デ・ハビエル（ザビエル）と出会うこととなった。それが、周知のように、イグナチオのソルボンヌ入学の12年後にイエズス会となる最初の核を形成することとなった。

ファーブルとザビエルの後に、他の4人の仲間たちがこのグループに加わった。ディエゴ・ライネス、アルフォンソ・サルメロン、ニコラス・デ・ボバディリア、シモン・ロドリゲスである。今は、このグループの生活のことにとどまらないし、その働きの内的な手がかりとなるものの分析をしないし、アルカラの最初のグループとも比較しない。今ここでは、イグナチオの回心のプロセスで、新たな局面が加わったことを述べれば十分である。それは、ゆっくりと静かだが、他のすべてのことと調和的で、教会における新たなカリスマを形づくっていった。

このグループは、パリ郊外モンマルトルのサン・ドニ聖堂の式で、勉学の後も共にとどまるという約束を固め、もし状況が許すならば、エルサレムに共に赴くことを約束した。あの1534年8月15日には彼らの誰も想像することはできなかったが、6年後に彼らは教皇パウロ三世に跪き教会における新たなグループとして認められることを願った。それは新しい修道会（またもう一つの！）であり、自分たちの予期せぬ場所に教皇から遣わされた者として派遣されることになるのである。

恐らく1535年4月上旬にパリを離れるとき、それは故郷のアスペイティアへの行程で、また他のさらなる別れだが、イグナチオは、エルサレムでの痛ましい挫折として過去12年間生きてきたことの実りを思い起こしていたであろう。仲間たちが借りてくれたラバにまたがり、もう

彼のものではない道程を導いていた隠された摂理の働きとして、聖地への意志に反して強いられた出発を思い起こしていた。

　地理的で時間的な距離からは、かのフランシスコ会管区長マルコス・デ・サロディオ神父は、イグナチオにとって、彼を驚かしてやまない神の構想の一部のように思われた。

　エルサレムにとどまるという彼の固い決意の挫折と終焉は、パリでの実り多い勉学期、とりわけその生涯と歴史に最終的にとどまる「主における友たち」のグループにおいてよみがえることになる。

2.6　第六段階　「世界とその事柄への回心」

　「世界とその事柄」への回心とよぶこのプロセスを最後にしたのは、イグナチオの霊的かつ神秘的なプロセスでも霊操でシステマティックに提示されているものも、このイグナチオ的な観点から主の弟子であるかを見分ける、すべての人格を向けることを望む目的への扉となると思われたからである。

　以前の回心では、イグナチオは、生きる密度、イエスとの親しさ、心の貧しさ、「他者」の媒介としての他者へと自らの生涯を転換し、世界とその事柄へと戻ることなしに深い転回を体験した。この回心は何から成るのか？

　出発点。恐らくはある聖人たちの模範に触発されて、イグナチオは、当初は、世を離れること、徹底的な隠遁への傾きを感じた。何か彼の中で、世界の放棄、「世界からの解放」を執拗に勧めるかのようだった。そして、「世界からの逃避（Fuga mundi）」の霊的な潮流の一部となることを望んだ。それは、修道会の禁域の沈黙か世俗の喧噪のすべての徴候から離れた洞窟のようなところで、命の真の感覚、平和、そしてそのすべてとともに神と出会うことへと促しているようだった。

　自叙伝のテキストを見ると、こう述べられている。「エルサレムから帰ってきたら ［…］ どうしたらよいだろうかと考えているうち、セビリアの厳律カルトゥジオ会の大修道院に入る考えが浮かんできた。そこへ

名も告げずに行けば、人々はきっと卑しい者として扱うだろうから」（自叙伝12番）、ブルゴスのミラフローレスのカルトゥジオ会の会則について情報を得るために、イニゴはロヨラから家の使用人を送り、「その結果は満足するに足るものであったが」（自叙伝12番）、この選択肢はすでに可能性からはほど遠いものと考えたので、それ以上心にとめることはなかった。

彼の内面の時間と空間を占めていたのは孤独の追求で、それは人間的なやり方の構造や手段とのいかなる接触も無くすほどに、神への無邪気な信頼のうちに自分の生活の計画をたてようとするほどだった。宮廷の会計と予算に慣れ親しんでいたので、イグナチオは、別の極端になり、金銭とのすべての起きうる接触を避けた。豊かさの中で生きることに慣れ親しんでいたので、明日のことは準備せずに、今日を生きることを好んだ。名声や認知されること（今日いうところの、インスタグラムやツイッターのフォロワー）に慣れ親しんでいたので、今はあまりにも知られすぎている公の舞台から身を引くという仕方で姿を消すことへの真摯な望みに委ねることを好んだ。

マンレサでのこの敬虔な隠者の段階は、人格的なプロセスに必要だった。だが、まもなく理解したのは、それがまだある途上の一つの停留所に過ぎないこと、また聖霊が苦行や過度の無分別な厳格さを超えた意味の別の地平にまで引き寄せているということだった。

どのようにしてこの変容はもたらされたのだろうか？　世から逃避への当初の望みから世界とその事柄を転倒させるようなイエズス会という組織への変容はどのように理解すべきだろうか？　すべては1522年8月と思われる、河岸沿いでの敬虔な散策に始まった。

「カルドネルの照らし」として知られているかの体験についてはほとんど知られていない。認識的かつ知性的な体験として、イグナチオは、「すべてのものが新しく感じられた」（自叙伝30番）と理解した、形而上学的―神秘的な直観に到った。イグナチオに尋ねてみたいのは、その「新しさ」は一体どこにあるのか、あの午後にかつて見たことのないも

ののうちに一体何を見たのかである。

　ロヨラを出発して数か月のまだ早い時期には、イグナチオはカルドネ
ル河に向かって座っている間に起きたことを理解していなかった。その
生涯に痕跡を残し、30年後にローマで原初的でインスピレーションを
あたえるものとして記憶されるような様々な体験の一つとなったのだが。

　私見では、このカルドネルの体験は、イグナチオ的―イエズス会的な
カリスマの中心的で構造的な要素の一つに歴史的―神秘的な基盤をすえ
るものである。すなわち、世界、その事柄と人びとに対する構成的な選
択、歴史と時間、その中で起こったこと、そして何よりもそこに住まう
人たちの選択である。

　歳月の流れとともに、イグナチオは、世界の解釈の仕方において展開
してきた。それは、世界に対する不信、疑念、あるいは一定の恐れを含
むような当初のまなざしから、世界を霊的な体験の欠かすことのできな
い要素として含むことになったのである。イエスに従うことは、世界を
自らと共に変容すること、自らのキリスト教的な責任の聖霊論的な場と
して世界を引き受けることを含んでいる。世界とその事柄と人びとの多
様性は、常に何か新しいものである。「すべてが新しく感じられる」こ
と（自叙伝30番、カルドネル）とその新しさは、そこに住まうすべての
もの、それを支えるすべてのものへの愛に満ちた神的な基盤となってい
る。

　イグナチオは、世界と創造主とのこの再結合、あるいは神性と世界の
ものとのこの絆に関して含意されている霊的な神学を少しずつ練りあげ
ていった。神は世界を見て、世界を見ながら世界を愛する、またそこに
住まうもの、新たな意味をあたえるものそのすべてを愛する。

　これまで述べてきたことのより深い理解のために、ここで二つの手が
かりとなることをごく短く指摘したい。第一のものはイグナチオが霊操
316番の段落で提示している慰めの定義の第一部の第二の構成要素の手
がかりとなる。イグナチオはこう付け加える。慰めというのは、「結果
として地上の造られたいかなるものも、それ自体においてではなく、そ

のすべてのものの創造者において愛することができるようになることである。」

　イグナチオにとって、神の愛の直接的な体験として慰めを体験することで、世界とその事柄に対して必要かつ直接的に向かうことになる。そのように神の愛によって獲得されるということは、世界とその事柄、そしてそのすべての事柄（「地上の造られたいかなるもの」）に愛をもって結ばれるということを意味する。というのは、慰めという手がかりによれば、究極的な一致と真実において、わたしを支え、基盤となっている愛そのものによって住まわれているわたしとして、被造物がわたしたちに提供されるからである。

　他の仕方ではありえないように、世界とその事柄への転回を正当化するもう一つの手がかりは、霊操を締めくくる愛に到るための観想（霊操230-237番）に見いだされる。神は、この世界に住み、働き、労働する。これが到達点である。1517年のあの第一の回心以来、イグナチオは、二つの根本的な現実を統合してきたのである。それは神と世界である。和解不可能な弁証法の二つの構成要素として提示されたりするのではなく、イエスとのふさわしいかかわりが、世界の創造的な次元に深く入ることへと穏やかにイグナチオを導いてゆくのである。それは、歴史の進行しつつある神化において、「わたしの持っていて、所有するすべてのもの」（霊操234番）をかかわらせるためである。こうして、イエスとの親しさから生まれたミッション（霊操98番：永遠の王）は、世界に向けられる。その世界には、神自身が、聖霊とともにすべてを満たしながら、待っているのである。

結論　「振り返り、益となる」ための五つのポイント

＋イグナチオの体験がわたしたちにしめしているのは、神と人間は、時として異なる解釈をするということである。人間にとって根本的な挫

折（傷）と読めることも、神にとっては意味に満ちた新たな生の始まりとなりうるのである。

+イグナチオの回心は、わたしたちの聖霊に対する抵抗よりも、神の恵みの力が常により大きいとみなす楽観主義でわたしたちを満たす。

+イグナチオの回心は、わたしたちが、絶えざる構築のうちにあり、聖霊によって沈黙のうちに築きあげられるプロセスにあると、自らをみなすようにわたしたちを励ます。聖霊の論理は、時としてわたしたちが見いだすのではなく、振り返ってみて明らかにされ、こうして一人ひとりへの神の愛に満ちたかけがえのない秘義を見いださせる。

+イグナチオの回心は、忍耐と慈しみをもって自らを見るようにわたしたちを招き、神の時間とプロセスのうちに入るように助ける。その時計はしばしばわたしたちのとは違うリズムで進むのである。

+イグナチオの回心は、最終的に、「慰め」から生きるようにわたしたちを励ます。それは、わたしたちの心の奥底にイエスによって告げ知らされたみ言葉、意味の危機にあってはこだまのようにとどまる唯一無二のみ言葉、また信仰の闇にあって記憶の光のようである。

（邦訳：川中　仁）

イグナチオ・ロヨラの回心とそのサイコスピリチュアルな見方

● 酒井陽介

　2021 年、イエズス会は、創立者聖イグナチオ・ロヨラ（1491-1556）の回心五百周年を祝った。しかし、この記念の年は、イグナチオの偉業に焦点をあてるという表面的な祝祭ではない。16 世紀のヨーロッパに生き、後に聖人となった一人の人間の回心の出来事を通して、私たちが、時代と文化を超え、今に至るまで紡がれた普遍的なメッセージと洞察を現代の日本に生きる私たちの日常に見出せるかが問われている。この機会に、人間イグナチオの回心の体験とその後の霊的遍歴が、如何にして「すべてのものをキリストにおいて新しく見る」体験になったのかを、哲学や神学に比べると、ずっと新しい学問体系の心理学の視点を借りながら見ていく。

　イグナチオ・ロヨラの霊性の特徴は、その成立の背景上、神秘的かつ経験的であり、実践的なものである。さらに、こころの動き（情動）や感情（情緒）を大切にする。イグナチオ自身が、『霊操』の中で言っているように、彼が大事にしたのは、「霊魂を充たし満足させるのは、多くを知ることではなく、ものごとを内的に感じ味わうこと」である（霊操 2 番）[1]。イグナチオの霊性、特に識別のプロセスは、こころの内側を覗き込むことなので、心理学とは、その意味で、相性がいいと言えるかもしれない。言ってみれば、それは、ものを悟り、内的に味わうという「プロセス」を重視している霊性である。イグナチオの回心は、何より

1　イグナチオ・デ・ロヨラ『霊操』川中仁訳・解説、2023参照。以下、霊操の引用は、こちらからの出典とする。

もまず、戦場での身体の傷とその結果もたらされた、こころに深く刻まれた痛みから始まった。そして、こころの痛みは、彼の魂をさらなる渇きへと導いた。

　このイグナチオ年にCannonball moment（被弾の瞬間）という言葉をよく耳にする。しかし、一発の砲弾が、すぐに霊的体験を引き起こしたのではない。被弾の体験は、人生のターニングポイントに過ぎない。新カトリック大事典によると「回心」は、「人間の全人格をもってする神に対する根本的な関係の変革である。人間が神の招きを自由に受け入れて、人格的に決断して行く信仰行為」とある。数年前に、列聖されたニューマン枢機卿は、次の言葉を残している。*"To live is to change, and to be perfect is to have changed often."* [2] すなわち、「生きるとは、変化することであり、完成とは、変化し続ける結果を言う」。この言葉は、回心のプロセスを端的に伝えている。

　特に欧米において、キリスト教の回心と言うと、信仰生活から離れている人々が、何かのきっかけで、悔い改めて、信仰の真理に改めて覚醒するという意味合いが強い。しかし、多くの日本人は、キリスト教文化を生活環境の全般に感じる中に生活していない。キリスト教が従来の生活様式や文化に根付いている欧米と、日本を取り巻くコンテクストには、随分と違いがある[3]。日本では、青年期以降の人たちが、自ら選んで信仰生活に入る場合が多く、それは、従来の西欧的な回心の内容とは異なり、どちらかといえば、若松英輔氏が言うところの「霊性の自覚」[4]と言

2　J. H. NEWMAN, *An Essay on the Development of Christian Doctrine* (1845) sect. 2.
3　例えば、日本の明治期の代表的なキリスト者に内村鑑三がいる。彼の回心のプロセスは、日本の発展を思愛国心故に、キリスト教信仰（文明）の理想化から始まり、キリスト教国（アメリカ）社会の現実への失望、利己心の苦悩、そして深い信仰を生きる師との出会いとキリストの贖罪の啓示体験を経ての日本観の変化というように、日本の土壌というコンテクストが不可欠である。欧米人が、彼の体験を理解するのは難しいだろう。特に、彼が、自身のキリスト教信仰を「武士道の上に接木されたる基督教」と呼んでいることからわかるように、明治に至る日本の文化的コンテキスト理解が不可欠であり、それは、従来のキリスト教文化圏における回心とも異なる。佐藤明『内村鑑三の信仰と日：余は如何にして基督信徒となりし乎』（法政大学紀要79、1-12頁）参照。
4　若松英輔『内村鑑三　悲しみの使徒』8頁。

う方が腑に落ちる気がする。西欧的な真理への目覚めとは異なる、霊性の自覚である入信の決意は、西欧的な従来のキリスト教的な回心体験という観点では、十分に説明しきれない[5]。

　近年、ヨーロッパにおいては、圏外からの移民によって新しい生活様式や宗教がもたらされ、同時に抗うことのできない世俗化により、伝統的なキリスト教的価値観は薄れ、信仰生活のありようは変わりつつある。その代わりに、霊的体験の新しいアプローチが求められている状況で[6]、ヨーロッパでは、「新福音化」や「新求道期間」が声高に叫ばれてきた。それは、教会への不信や押し寄せる世俗化、そして非キリスト教系移民の移住などにより、変化が迫られる従来のキリスト教文化とアイデンティティの危機を背景にしているとも考えられる[7]。しかし、今回、私たちに投げかけられている問いは、単に、遠ざかっていた信仰から覚醒するという回心物語の分かち合いではなく、より多層で豊かな回心のプロセスに注目することである。

　こうした背景の中、キリスト教文化圏である欧米のみならず、世界は、「新福音化」よりも福音化に先立つ、「新予備福音化」（New Pre-Evangelization）の必要性があるとするイエズス会の神学者マイケル・ポール・ギャラハ神父（Michael Paul Gallagher, S.J. 1939-2015）の考え[8]を紹介する。「新予備福音化」とは、ギャラハ神父によれば、「キリストという驚きに備えて人々に同伴すること」である。言ってみれば、キリストが説く新しい教えに人々を導いた洗礼者ヨハネの役割のようなものである。彼はさらに続ける。「イエズス会には、神による驚きの入り口へ

5　欧米の自我の意識とは異なることは、例えば日本の民話や昔話を見るとそのコントラストがよくわかる。河合隼雄『昔話と日本人の心』参照。

6　K. VALENTA, *The Church in the West is in decline-and nationalism won't save it*, In *America The Jesuit Review* (July 15 2021) 参照。

7　例えば、最近の例によれば、現ヨーロッパ司教協議会会長のJean Claude Hollerich枢機卿は、コロナ後の教会において、信仰を実践する信徒は "will be smaller in number, because all those who no longer came to Mass, because they came only for cultural reasons, these 'cultural Catholics' of the left and the right, will no longer come." （Cardinal predicts Church, Europe will be 'weaker' after pandemic, ELISE ANN ALLEN, *Crux*, September 4, 2020より）

8　Jesuits in Ireland (https://www.jesuit.ie/videos/michael-paul-gallagher-sj/) 参照。

と続く、長く、ゆっくりと時間をかけた、人間的かつ霊的な旅路を同伴する伝統がある」と。これは、まさにイグナチオ・ロヨラ自身の回心のプロセスに起因するものであり、言ってみれば、イグナチオの霊性の特色である。それは、恩寵に応えたり、抗ったりして生きる人間への理解に満ち、その中にあって識別し、前に歩みを進める同伴の伝統である。現イエズス会総長アルトゥーロ・ソーサ神父も、その著書で次のように言っている。「キリスト者の人生は、巡礼である。自分自身から出て、歩み出し、導かれ、同伴され、驚きへと開かれるのである」。巡礼とは、予想や期待を超えてキリストに出会うのだということである[9]。イグナチオもまた、彼の予想を大きく超えて、キリストに出会った。そうであるなら、私たちの役割は、生きている日常と現実に顕現するキリストと出会えるように、人々とともに歩むことである。付加価値として新たな取り組みも大切だが、それ以上に、生きている現実と取り巻く環境の中に神の存在と神からの呼びかけを探し、感じることを福音化に先立つ事柄は、大切にしている。日本の社会そして教会も、まだ全体として、予備福音化を共通の課題として取り組まないといけないと思う。

　キリストを通して新しい眼を得るのは、まず、自分のあり様と現実を見つめないことには始まらない。そして、これこそが、回心の始まりなのである。今回のイグナチオの回心の体験を通して、新しい眼を持つ呼びかけは、私たちの生きている日常の現実の中で、キリストとの出会いや語らいを体験できるという促しなのである。ベネディクト16世もかつてこう言った。「回心ははっきりとした決定的なことがらです。しかし、わたしたちはこの根本的な決断を成長させなければなりません。すなわち、わたしたちの生涯全体を通してそれを実現しなければなりません」（2008年1月一般謁見演説）。回心は、一度きりの出来事ではなく、歩み行く道・プロセスであることを、意識しながらイグナチオの回心の歩みの中にその可能性を見ていきたい。

9　A. Sosa, *In Cammino con Ignazio*, 19頁。

本来、心理学は、その性質上、信仰、教義そして、霊的体験の実証に関係しない。しかし、心理学は、個人または集団の心理的現実のコンテクストにおいて、信じるとはいったいどういう意味を持つかの理解を深めることに役立つ。神学者で人間の成長と信仰の関係性について研究したジェイムズ・ファウラー（James Fowler 1940-2015）は次のように言う。「信仰とは、（中略）全人的な方向性であり、人の持つ希望や、努力、思考や、行動に目的を与えるものである」。それゆえに「信仰は、人の性格や人格のなくてはならない部分である」[10]。ここで述べられているように、人間の成長・発達と信仰には有意な関係がある。宗教的回心は、人が、信じ、帰依し、実践するプロセスである[11]。その意味で、宗教的回心を考えるためには、予定調和ではない人間性を誠実に見つめ、人と神の邂逅の出来事を省察する必要がある。

　近年、サイコスピリチュアリティという分野が注目されている。人間のこころを扱う心理学が、同時に、超越的な存在との関係や霊的な価値観も扱うのである。信仰と心理学は対峙するどころか、神のみ前に生きる人間理解のために看過できない関係にあることがわかってきている。実は、これは決して新しい考えではなく、神学者聖トマス・アクィナスは、13世紀に *Gratia non tollit naturam, sed perficit.*（ST, I, I, 8 ad 2）、すなわち、恩寵は自然を廃さず、かえって完成するという有名な定義を述べている。さらに、「神の栄光は、生きている人間」と、教父聖イレネオの言葉も示すように、被造物としての人間性において神の栄光と恩寵が示現する。心理学というものが、知られるよりもずっと以前の16世紀に、イグナチオ・ロヨラは、自分のこころの動きと陰に陽に働きかける霊を認識し、人生選定と神のみ旨を見出す祈りの仕方を体系化した。かつて、聖パウロが、私は弱い時にこそ強いと言ったように、人間は、己が強さが崩れ落ち、弱く、脆い自分を認める時、超越的な存在から与えられる力を意識することができる。聖アゥグスチヌスも「あなたはわ

10　J. FOWLER, *Stages of Faith*, 14, 92頁参照。
11　R. F. PALOUTZIAN, *Religious Conversion and Spiritual Transformation,* 331頁。

たしたちを、ご自身にむけてお造りになりました。ですからわたしたちの心は、あなたのうちに憩うまで、安らぎを得ることができないのです」（『告白』1, 1, 59頁）と言っている。それは現代で言えば、人が、人生に疑問や息詰まりを感じ、霊的同伴やカウンセリングを受ける時、自己との出会いだけではなく、まだはっきりとわからなくとも自己のうちに自分を超えた存在を意識し始めることと似ている。

　宗教心理学者ウイリアム・ジェイムズによれば、回心とは、統一感を欠き、分裂していた自己が、超越的な存在との出会いを通じて、幸福であることを意識し、新しい自己に生まれ変わることである[12]。例えば、分析的な心理学[13]の観点から言えば、成人期の回心の場合、パーソナリティの特質は、大きく変化はしない[14]。宗教的回心の後に起こるのは、気質の変化というより、各々の気質の取る表現の仕方の変化である。すなわち、生きる目的、価値基準、態度、信念、アイデンティティに新しい意味を見出すようになる[15]。イグナチオの回心を経ての自己実現は、確かに、彼の「肥大化した自我の死」という戦場と病床で負った挫折の体験から始まった変容のプロセスだった。その後、彼は、新しい生きる目的、価値基準、態度、信念、アイデンティティをキリストとの出会いと交わり（神秘的なコミュニケーション）を通して、形成していった。

　宗教的回心の体験は、霊的変容をもたらす[16]。霊的変容のプロセスで

12　ウイリアム・ジェイムズ『宗教的経験の諸相』上、238頁。

13　『宗教心理学』の著者エドウィン・スターバック（Edwin Starbuck1866-1947）によれば、回心の適齢期は16歳頃の思春期で、そこには、精神的覚醒よりも罪からの脱出という動機が強いという。続く心理学者たちがと唱えた、例えば、ユングのミッドライフ・クライシス、エリクソンのアイデンティティ・クライシス、そしてマズローのピークエクスペリエンスとの関連も考えられる（新カトリック大事典、p.1017s参照）。例えば、堀江宗正は、次のように書いている。「マズローにおいても、ユングにおいても、自我とは他なるもの——マズローの場合は、他者や世界などの対象、ユングの場合は自我を保証するような内容を持つ無意識的イメージ——が自我に直面し、それによって自我が崩れるような体験が、自己実現の重要な契機となる。」（『歴史の中の宗教心理学』51頁）

14　Costa &McCrae, 1994, *Set Like Plaster? Evidence for the Stability of Adult Personality*. In T. F. Heatherton & J. L. Weinberger (Eds.), *Can Personality Change?* Washington, DC: American Psychological Association 参照。

15　R. Paloutzian, *Religious Conversion and Spiritual Transformation*, In *Handbook of Psychology of Religion and Spirituality*, 332－333頁。

は、願い、信じることと現実との間のギャップである「なるべき」と「である」の葛藤が起こる[17]。霊的変容は、このギャップに生じる葛藤を抜きにしては、ありえない。人生の大切な問いかけがなされている時、今まで持っていた自分の意味の捉え方では、太刀打ちできないので、時に、人は、この体験の中、信仰を離れる場合もあるほどである。望まない結果や、苦しい体験の中で、もがきながら、人は、新しい意味を見出すことで、乗り越えようとする。若きイグナチオは、パンプローナの戦いにおいて、自分たちが、勝つべきものと信じて疑わなかった。しかし、敗戦を喫し、それも敵の大砲により被弾し、戦地を退くという屈辱を味わった。それでも、イグナチオは、再び、宮廷での立身出世と猛々しく戦場で活躍する自分を思い描きながら、被弾した足の全快を願い、祈ったことであろう。しかし、手術は、思いのほか難しく、元のようには戻らなかった。自分の我を押し通せないところに行きつく現実の最中にあって、彼は、徐々に「こうあるべき」から「これである」という自分の現実を受け入れ始め、それでも前に進もうとする時、こころに語りかける超越的存在を徐々に意識し始めた。若きイグナチオは、生きるための意味の転換を迫られたのである。「こうあるべき」という思い込みは、柔軟なこころ持ちを阻み、自分のありようを謙虚に認め、神からの新しさへの招きに開かれるのを邪魔する悪い霊の仕業。反対に、「これである」とありのままを認めることは、神からの霊の促しであり、そこから変化・成長する契機になる。それが、イグナチオ・ロヨラの体験した霊動の葛藤の始まりだった。こう考えると、イグナチオの体験は、心理学の発想とそう遠いところにはないのである。

　宗教的テーマを心理学、特に精神分析の観点から取り組んだイエズス会司祭で分析家のウィリアム・マイスナー（W.W. Meissner, S.J. 1931-2010）[18] は、精神分析をイグナチオの霊性に掛け合わせて、何ができる

16　同上、334頁。

17　P. C. HILL, *Spiritual Transformation: Forming the Habitual Center of Personal Energy*. In *Research in the Social Scientific Study of Religion* (Vol.4, pp. 159-182 (2002)) 参照。

のかと問われた時、こう答えた。それは、イグナチオの霊的視点をより
よく理解するためであり、イグナチオの考え方をより深く探ることで、
彼の霊的な成長と人間的努力の一側面を理解することができるのである[19]。
それゆえに、彼は、聖人の偉業の霊的・宗教的側面よりも、聖人を取り
巻く環境や他者との人間関係、そして聖人の霊的あゆみにおける人間的
動機、葛藤、発達上の影響や生きる目的に、より大きな関心を持ってい
る[20]。そうすることで、より深みのある人間イグナチオが私たちの前に
現れるということである。今回、私がしているのは、その試みの延長に
あるようなものである。

　自己とは、人生の物語の産物である。ここでは、イグナチオの人生の
物語に入り込むことによって、可能な限り、彼の深みと、彼の生きた価
値観や徳を探り、明らかにしようと思う[21]。イグナチオが書き残した文
書または彼に関する公式の文書は、大きく分けると6種類[22]あるが、こ

18　オスカー・フィスター（Oskar Pfister）やウイリアム・ジェイムズ（William James）は、宗教
　　心理学または、信仰と心理学の研究の先駆けである。フィスターに至っては、フロイトの直弟
　　子の一人であり、プロテスタント牧師の分析家である。彼とフロイトの手紙は、分析的なアプ
　　ローチの宗教心理学を知る上で、非常に重要な資料である。TILMAN HABERMAS & CYBÉLE DE
　　SILVEIRA, *The Development of Global Coherence in Life Narratives across Adolescence*, In
　　Developmental Psychology, 44 (3), 707-721 (2008) によると、人間の成長に関する主観的な説明
　　とその人のパーソナリティとの間の有意な関連性は、フロイトによるヒステリーの症例に関す
　　る研究（1905年）のように臨床家によって研究され、個人に関する包括的な情報源として自伝
　　的資料を使用する根拠としてパーソナリティ心理学者（ALLPORT, 1942; MCADAMS & PALS,
　　2006）によって研究されてきた。その中でも、ルターやガンディーに関するエリクソンの研究
　　は、主観的なライフストーリーの展開が成熟した心理的アイデンティティの達成と有意に関連
　　していることを示した最初の詳細な研究である。707頁参照。
19　W. W. MEISSNER, *Transformative Processes in the Spiritual exercises*, In *Psyche and Spirit Dialectics
　　of Transformation* (W. W. MEISSNER and CHRIS R. SCHLAUCH) University Press of America,
　　2003, 120頁。
20　MEISSNER, *Psychoanalytic Hagiography: The Case of Ignatius of Loyola* (*Theological Studies* 52,
　　1991, 3頁)
21　D. MCADAMS, *The Psychology of The Life Stories*, In *Review of General Psychology*, 5 (2), 100-122
　　(2001) 参照。マクアダムズは、ナラティブと人生の研究には、概ね共通する6つの原則がある
　　という。1）自己が語られる。2）物語は、有意に人生をまとめあげる。3）物語は、社会的関係
　　性の中で語られ、社会的現象として理解される。4）物語は、時間とともに変わる。5）物語は、
　　文化的テクストである。6）ある物語は、道徳的観点を伝える優れた内容を持つ。イグナチオの
　　物語にも、こうした特質は見られる。

の中で、イグナチオ自身が回心の体験に触れているのは、『自叙伝』である。第一資料としての『自叙伝』には、留意すべき点もある。第一に、この自伝は、弟子のカマラ神父によって口述筆記されたものである[23]。ただ、カマラの編集の余地が全くないとも言えない。別言すれば、信憑性の問題である。『ロヨラのイグナチオその自伝と日記』[24] の序文で、イグナチオの霊性の専門家で、かつて日本にも暮らしたフランシスコ・オスーナ神父は、興味深い言葉を記している。「イグナチオは、自分の青年時代の軽薄な生活について、詳細に、しかも明確に他の時代と区別してカマラ師に語ったにもかかわらず、この最初の 26 年間は、わずか数行に短縮されてしまった。イグナチオを尊敬するあまりか、それともこの物語のプランを壊さないためか、とにかくわれわれの興味をそそる当時の逸話や出来事は、永遠に世に知られなくなってしまったわけである」（10頁）。カマラは、若い頃からイグナチオを理想化する傾向も強かったと言われている[25]。いずれにしても、イグナチオの人生の歩みを知る上で、自叙伝に勝る生の声が聞けるナラティブはない。そこには、回心の体験を経た悩み多き青年イグナチオと、後に巡礼者と自称する彼の歩みが刻まれている。ここからは、彼を改名前の本名であるイニゴと呼ぶことにする。それでは、特にロヨラとマンレサにおける若きイニゴの回心の物語に少し分け入る。

---

22 イグナチオが書き残した文書または彼に関する公式の文書は、大きく分けると次の6つある。まずは、『霊操』である。さらにイエズス会の統治と法規に関する書『イエズス会会憲』。そして、今回、取り上げる『自叙伝』である。次に挙げるのは、数多く残っているイグナチオの書いた手紙類であり、これは総長として世界中に派遣された会員との連絡の記録であり、決定事項の通達であり、相談への返信である。さらに、『イグナチオの霊的日記』と呼ばれるものがあり、総長としてローマ滞在時代の様々な霊的体験が記されている。最後に、彼の列聖調査の時に残された公式文書がある。

23 L. G. D. CAMARA『メモリアル』、356頁（バラ訳『イグナチオの日々を見た弟子の覚え書き』）。

24 A. エバンヘリスタ、佐々木孝訳編、1966、桂書房。

25 カマラのこの特質について次のように書かれている。「イグナチオにもありうる短所には気づかない。気づいたにしても、イグナチオを理想化する基準に照らしてその短所を解釈する。（中略）共に生活する会員の目に聖人を遠く感じさせるほどに不自然な彼の態度、生来の懸命さゆえの結果なのか、それとも打算による見せかけに過ぎないものか、場合によってはかなり不分明なイグナチオの態度をカマラは見分けることができない。」（ダ・カマラ著、ホセ・ミゲル・バラ編訳『イグナチオの日々を見た弟子の覚え書き』の序文より12頁、J. M. GRANERO, *"El Memorial" de Camara, Manresa* 39 (1967), 75頁)

イニゴの出自を語る上で、バスクという土地について少し説明を加えておく必要がある。バスク人は、独立心と忠誠心、言ってみれば、個と集団といった一見すると相反する価値観を内包する複雑な心理を持っている。バスクには、大洋に繰り出す船乗りが多いとも言われ、また山間で暮らす力自慢の森の民として土地に根付く愛郷心も強いのも特徴である。海と山の異なる自然環境を併せ持ち、古来よりそれらを利用し、たくましく生き、独特な生活文化を営んできた。こうしたバスクの自然的、歴史的風土が、そこに息づく人々に与える影響は、計り知れない[26]。その意味でイニゴは、特有の文化とその時代の影響を受けた誇り高きバスクの一人だった。もしかしたら、この地理的、文化的特性が彼のこころの内に生じる、相反する二つの力のコントラストに気づくことに何らかの影響を与えたかもしれない。さらに、個と集団のミッションの緊張関係など、現代でも問われるイエズス会の特質に通じるテーマがあるようにも思える。

　次に、イニゴが生まれた当時のロヨラ家は、どのような状況だったのかを見てみよう。彼は、バスクはギプスコアにある貴族ロヨラ家に父ベルトランと母マリアナの13人兄姉の末っ子として1491年に生を受けた。生後まもなくして、洗礼を受けオーニャの聖イニゴの洗礼名を授かった。カスティーリャ王国に仕えるこの一族は、小さいながらに代々の名門であり、末っ子であったイニゴには、家督を継ぐプレッシャーはないものの、当然のことながら子どもたちは、ロヨラ家の名に恥じないように生きていく期待や価値観が植え付けられたと考えられる。それは、イニゴの自我に避けられぬ影響を与えたと考えるのが自然である。

　母マリアナは、イニゴが、まだ幼い時に亡くなった。彼は、7歳まで村の女性に預けられ、育てられた。7歳になると、兄のマルティンが結婚し、義姉となるマグダレーナが城に来る。イニゴは、城に戻され、以

26　作家の司馬遼太郎は、バスク人について次のように言う。「彼らは、愛国者であっても、劣等感の裏返しにすぎない国粋主義者ではないのである。このあたりが、バスクの山水の美しさとともに、バスク人の気持ちのいいところだと思った。」(『街道を行く　南蛮のみちⅠ』)

後、16歳で小姓になって居城を出るまでマグダレーナが、いわば母親代わりとなる。このマグダレーナが、後にイニゴの人生、特に回心の契機に深く関わる。親を早くに亡くした子どもへの影響は、少なからずあるものと思われる。特に絶対的な愛情と信頼の対象である母親を早く亡くし、さらに家からも離れて暮らさなければいけなかった少年イニゴの心境は、どれほどの喪失感や痛みがあっただろうか。亡くなった母親への強い思慕や母親代わりの対象への愛着などが、青年期のイニゴの女性への関わりや愛着に、その複雑で不安定な心象が見え隠れしているようである。

　「彼は 26 歳の時まで世俗の虚栄におぼれていた。特に、むなしい大きな名誉欲をいだき、武芸に喜びを見出していた」（自叙伝 1 番）と書いてある。父の死後、15、6 歳の頃、イニゴは、宮廷の会計監査の責任者であったホアン・ベラスケスの小姓となる。住み慣れた緑豊かなバスクを離れ、荒涼としたカスティーリャに向かった若いイニゴのこころに、何らかの「欠けた」感覚が芽生えても不思議ではなく、その欠けた部分を埋め合わせるのが、のちに彼の中で野心となる宮廷での煌びやかな生活であったと想像するのは難くない[27]。小姓としての素養を身に付けながら、生活を謳歌し、決闘、賭け事そして女性と、野心の実現と欲得にものを言わせ暮らしていた。同時に王の妹君インファンタ・カタリーナへの身分の違う恋慕に胸を焦がした。1517 年に主君ベラスケスが亡くなると、今度は、根っからの軍人であるナバラ総督アントニオ・デ・マンリケの元に移った。宮廷生活ではなく、戦場が、イニゴの生きる場になっていく。1521 年にナバラでのフランス軍との戦いに行き着くのは、こうした背景がある。

　たいへん強固な自我を持っていたと思われるイニゴのパーソナリティを見る時、次の二つの傾向が顕著となる。彼には、強迫的（obsessive-compulsive）と自己愛的（narcissistic）の二つのパーソナリティスタイル

27　J. A. MUNITIZ, *St. Ignatius of Loyola and severe depression*, *The Way* 44/ 3 2005, 60頁参照。

の特徴が見られる。この二つの特徴あるスタイルは、彼の若かりし頃から晩年に至るまでの行動や態度にその片鱗を残していることからわかる。例えば、パンプローナの戦いは、イニゴのパーソナリティをよく示すものと言える。イニゴの自我理想に誇大性（優越感）と自己愛（ナルシシズム）が見られる[28]。マイスナーは、それを自己愛パーソナリティ的だと言う。その特徴は、高い理想である。大きなことを成したいと願う成功欲、万能感、不死身感、英雄的理想のために危険を冒すことへのためらいの無さ、そして不可能と思えることを乗り越えていこうとする前のめりの姿勢である。このパーソナリティの人は、通常時よりも、戦時など非常事態でその特質を発揮する[29]。

　ナバラ内戦の最後の戦いとなった、いわゆるパンプローナ蜂起に、イニゴは向かった。1521年5月20日、彼の地で右足を被弾した。被弾した武人イニゴは、故郷に錦を飾るどころか、敵兵の温情と介護を受け、居城のロヨラ城まで連れてこられる。勝ち損なうだけでなく、同時に死に損なった底知れぬ挫折感を味わったのではないだろうか。被弾で砕かれた右足は、早速の外科手術を必要としていた。容姿へのこだわりも人並み以上にあったイニゴにとり、なんとしても再び宮廷に仕え、戦場での勇猛な活躍のためには、どんな代償を払っても足を元通りにすることが最大の願いだった。麻酔のない時代の手術のこと、自叙伝には、手術中、一言も発することなく、かたく拳を握りしめ、耐え忍んだと書いてある。術後、接合した足の見た目に納得のいかないイニゴは、激しい痛みの伴う手術をもう一度願う。彼は、この時点で、まだ「あるべき」自

28　フロイトは、こうした心情を去勢恐怖と呼ぶ。
29　日本の歴史の中で、この特徴に共通した人物を思い出す。それは、織田信長である。ルイス・フロイスは著作『日本史』（*Historia de Japam*）の中で、信長については次のように書き残している。信長は、「きわめて稀に見る優秀な人物であり、非凡の著名なカピタン（司令官）として、大いなる賢明さをもって天下を統治した者であったことは否定し得ない。彼は中くらいの背丈で、華奢な体躯であり、ヒゲは少なく、はなはだ声は快調で、極度に戦を好み、軍事的修練にいそしみ、名誉心に富み、正義において厳格であった」。これは、単なる推測の域を出ないが、イニゴが被弾していなかったとしたら、その宗教性や信仰心は別として、信長のような人物になっていたかもしれない。当時、神仏を恐れず、絶対的な権力を目指した信長もまた、実は、自己愛の強い、去勢恐怖と戦った人生だったと言えるかと思う。

分が勝り、「そうである」自分の現実を受け入れられていない。その痛みに耐えるのであるから、並外れた意志の持ち主であったであろう。イニゴの目的に迷いなく突き進む決意、困難をものともしない勇敢さは、彼の強い自我理想のもう一面の姿である。ただ、この強靭な精神力をこの時点のイニゴは、自分の夢のため、自分で描いた再び手に入れたいと望んだ野心のため、言ってみれば、自己愛的な欲得を願ってのことだった。手術は、なんとか成功したが、やはり右足は、どうしても少し短くなった。彼が、以来、足を引きずるようにして歩くのにはこのわけがあった。

　術後、自由に歩き回れない彼は、することもなく、時間を持て余し、夢想に費やし、自分を鼓舞するため騎士物語を欲したが、信心深い義理の姉マグダレーナが、夫の不在の間に守っていたロヨラの城には、その類の本はなかった。代わりに、正反対の二冊の信心書が手渡される。それは、サクソニアのルドルフの書いた『イエス・キリスト伝（黄金伝説）』とイベリア半島で当時広く読まれていた『聖人たちの華』（Flos Sanctorum）だった。この二冊の本との出会いが、イニゴの人生に新たな方向性を与えていく。

　自叙伝には、イニゴの病床に聖母子が現れたとある。聖母子に、理想化された優しき義姉マグダレーナと自分を無意識的に見ていたとも言えるのではないだろうか。のちに、イグナチオは、敬愛を込めて聖母を「我らの貴婦人」（Nuestra Señora）と呼んでいた。母に代わり、自分を育てあげてくれたマグダレーナは、聖母を意識させる特別な存在であったのであろう。術後の回復期に、硬かった彼の自己愛的な自我は、父親の脅威の重圧にとって代わった優しく寛大で、信心深いマグダレーナとの関わりによって、徐々に和らいでいく。その意味で、ロヨラ城での日々は、起き上がることもままならないイニゴにとって、全幅の信頼を抱くことのできる、子どもがえりの時期でもあったのかもしれない。

　彼の回心の体験を理解する上で、この二つのパーソナリティスタイル

は不可欠な要因になっている。繰り返すが、恩寵は、自然を差しおかず、かえって仕上げる。人生の歩みを進めていくうちに、気質や人格に変化がなくても、その人特有の成熟したあり方と現実との折り合いの付け方を学ぶようになる。恩寵の働きのもと、彼の成熟のプロセスは、新しい形の自己をイニゴにもたらし始めた。しかし、あくまでも野心的なのである。当時としては、危険極まりないエルサレムに巡礼に行く。聖ドミニコが、聖フランシスコができるなら、自分にもできる[30]。二人の大聖人を引き合いに出すなど、相当に自我理想が強くなければ、出てこない発想である。それでは、この時のイニゴに起きた変化の興味深い特徴を見ていこう。

　かつて心躍らせた騎士物語の夢想は、段々と長続きせず、かえって気持ちが裏寂しくなり、不安になる。反対に、聖人たちの証しに想いを寄せると、力と慰めを感じる。彼は、模範とした聖人たちの証しを自我理想に取り入れた。この頃のイニゴの中では、かつて宮廷と戦場で培われた価値観と今回の新しく取り入れた価値観とが混在している状態と言える。そして、依然として外的な功績に囚われていて、自己愛的な視点がまだこの時点では、優っている。二つの霊の働きかけの間で揺れ動くこころの動きの違いは、言ってみれば、二つの価値観の違いの間における葛藤でもあった。はじめ、イニゴの自我は、新しく取り入れた霊的な価値観を古い自己愛に同化させ、この二つの異質の価値観を適度に和解させたように見える。しかし、キリストに従うという新しい価値観の理解が深まるにつれ、徐々にそれが不可能なことだと悟らざるを得なかったようである。強い自己愛と自己奉献は、相容れない緊張関係を生んだ。イニゴは、こうやって、自分の今までの人生の野心的価値観、自己愛的で、若気あふれる理想から、より潔く、高く、深い霊的な方向へと徐々に舵を切るようになる[31]。聖人の真似事ではなく、自分らしいあり方を

30　のちに『霊操』「教会と心を合わせるための規定」第一二則で、「わたしたち生きている者たちと過去の福者たちとを比較するのは慎まねばならない。」と書いている。これも若い頃の自身の反省にたっての言葉か。

見つけるのである。言い換えれば、イニゴにとっての新しい気づきと理解が、少しずつ現実と本当の理想に追いついていくのである。こうして、ドミニコでもない、フランシスコでもない、イニゴらしい霊性が生まれていく。

　自叙伝の中に「神はちょうど小学校の先生が子どもを教えるように彼を教え導いた」（自叙伝27番）と書かれている。小学生とあるが、実は幼児のようなものではなかったのだろうか。これを理解する助けとし、英国の分析家ウイニコットの「ほどよい母親」という概念を少し使ってみよう。ウイニコットによれば、生まれて間もない幼児は、不安の縁に立っている[32]。「ほどよい母親」は、幼児の欲求にできる限り適応し、幼児に、一体感と全能感を与える。そのうちに、幼児の能力が増大するにつれ、徐々に現実感を与えていくのである[33]。現実感とは、母親（養育者）は、幼児の要求に全て応えるわけではないということである。これをすることができる母親をウイニコットは、「ほどよい母」と呼んだ[34]。そうして、幼児は、徐々に、その一体感と全能感が、幻想であることを学ぶ。しかし、安心感を取り戻さなければ、幻滅した幼児は、生きていけない。幼児と母親との間に双方によって育まれる安心感を生む空間が必要である。この空間で、幼児の全能感が、破棄され、あらためて、現実の対象に対応し始める。こうして、全能感が通らない、もやもやした経験から、徐々に思うように、欲するようにいかない現実を把握し始める。ウイニコットは、この潜在的な空間を、内的な全能感と外的現実の中間領域（Intermediate area）だと言う。中間領域が、その本領を発揮するのは、受け入れ難い現実と向き合う際のクッションのような役割を果たすことである。そうして、現実に即した理性的な判断を助けてくれる。この時に、現実の世界に触れる前に、その中間領域で、安心を与え

31　MEISSNER, *Psychoanalytic Hagiography*, 32頁参照。
32　D. W. ウイニコット著、牛島定信訳『情緒発達の精神分析理論』1977、59頁。
33　ウイニコット著、橋本雅雄訳『遊ぶことと現実』1979、14頁。
34　同上、17頁。

るようなモノ、例えば、人形やおもちゃといった移行対象（transitional object）を必要とする。そこで行われる、母親との、そして移行対象との関係は、幼児に外界（世界）は、安心な場所であることを悟らせるのである。別言すれば、橋渡しのような役割を果たす場であり、時間なのである。この幼年期に培われる「初めての安心感」が、例えば、エリック・エリクソンの言う「基本的信頼」の役割を果たし、人間の成長発達に大いに関係すると考えられる[35]。

　少し専門的な言葉が出たが、イニゴの例に当てはめるとわかりやすいかもしれない。大怪我をし、夢に敗れたイニゴは、大いに幻滅し、体を動かすことさえできずに、ほぼ全ての世話を義姉マグダレーナをはじめとする他の人にしてもらわなければいけなかった。イニゴにとって、「ほどよい母」は、マグダレーナであり、そして回心の体験全体を通しては、神がその役割を果たしていたように考えられる。安心感は、慰め、そして幻滅は、荒み。イニゴは、これを人間関係でも、さらに霊の働きでも体験した。手厚い看護をしてくれた、母親がわりのマグダレーナに、暇つぶしのオモチャがわりの騎士物語を欲するも、断られ、代わりに全く興味のなかった霊的読書を充てがわれた。またしても幻滅体験。かつての野心と相まった全能感や優越感は、もやもやとしたものに変わっていく。例えば、イニゴにとっての全能感溢れる思い込みは、彼の中で肥大化したカトリックスペインであったり、過度に理想化されたカタリーナ妃であったり、夢の舞台である宮廷と戦場で活躍している自分だったり、さらに移行対象は、理想の先のフランシスコやドミニコであったりする。しかし、まだ現実には追いついていないのである。夢も野心も潰え、ロヨラでの療養の日々とマンレサは、被弾体験から巡礼者となる間の時間である。それは、青年イニゴが、新しい現実に向かい、巡礼者になる移行空間のようなものだっただろう。まだ見ぬ現実に向けて、自己の意識を修正していく時なのである。

35　奥田秀巳、〈信じる〉態度の基礎：基本的信頼の手がかりに、*Habitus*, 18: 131-143頁参照。

病床での「何もできない子どもがえり」の時間は、もう一度、イニゴが、いのちを取り戻し、生きがいを見つけるために、そして信頼を育むために、滋養豊かな苗床のような時間と場所になった。この時期は、あらためて感じる家族の愛と支えによって育まれた基本的な信頼が、絶望の淵にいたイニゴを支え、新しい可能性の満ちた世界が開かれていく。神もまた、迷えるイニゴに対し、近くから、時に遠くから時宜にかなった関わり、そして浄めのチャレンジと慰めを伴った同伴をした。

　私たちの人生にも、それぞれユニークなありようの中間領域がある。新しい現実を目の前にして、迷いながらも準備する時間である。現代では、コロナ・パンデミックの翻弄されるこの時間は、もしかすると人類共通の中間領域となっているかもしれない。ただ、ここで大切なのは、あくまでも中間領域は、永続するものではなく、そして、「移行対象」は、遅かれ早かれ、現実にとって代わるものである。あくまでも時が来ると、去りゆくもの、手放すものである。それに対してその執着（乱れた愛着）から自由になることを人間的な意味では、成長または発達と呼び、霊的な意味では霊的変容と呼ぶ。中間領域は、成熟に欠かせない体験だと言えるであろう。霊操155番にある、神によりよく奉仕することを選ぶ「第三種の人」の選択は、まさにそのことである。イニゴは、いつまでも小学生のようではなかった。巡礼者として自分の足で、歩いていくようになる。蛇足だが、キリストは、アルファであり、オメガである。私たちは、初めであり、終わりである神に守られ、その中間に生きている。私たちのこの世における命もまた、永遠の命を前にした有限な中間領域にあるのかもしれない。

　ジェイムズは、宗教心理学の古典『宗教的経験の諸相』の中で、回心という体験には、二つの極となるこころの状態があると指摘する。一方を、罪の意識、不完全さ、痛悔、そして自信の無さなどが占めている。もう一方には、新しく生まれ変わりたいという希望を抱く積極的な理想が秘められている。ただ、多くの場合、罪の意識が強く、負の影響力を

持ち、それが強迫観念になってしまう。こうした負の感情が強くなると、当然、罪悪感や不安感に取り憑かれ、感情も理性もそして身体も打ちひしがれてしまうのである。まさに、イニゴに起きた負の感情の連鎖と自死を思うまでに至った背景は、こうしてある程度の説明がつく。過去の過ちを取り消すのではなく、そのままの自分を差し出しながら、生きていくしかないのである。神が先に、彼を探し求めてくれているあわれみを体験的に知るほかないのである。

　完璧になろうとする中で、負のループに入ったイニゴの神経は荒み始めた。この背景には、彼が当時、持っていた神概念があるかもしれない。自分を追い詰めていく彼の姿を見ると、そこにあるのは、厳しい神のイメージである。それは、父親のイメージか、ロヨラ家という家の重圧によるものか、はたまた当時の国土回復運動の世相を反映してのことか、いずれにしても若きイニゴの抱いていた神のイメージは、正義の神であるけれど、どこか懲罰的で、小さな罪も見逃さない、どちらかといえば、恐るべき神だったのではないだろうか。ロヨラで、やさしき聖母子に見守られ、マグダレーナを通して、いつくしみ深い神の顔を彼は見ていたから、それだけではなかったと思う。このように、神概念における光と闇との緊張と変化が、彼の回心の体験の中にも見て取れる。例えば、イグナチオとマルチン・ルターの比較は、興味深い研究になると思われる。単純な比較はできないが、ほぼ同時代に生き、北ヨーロッパとイベリア半島のカトリックの文化的差異はあるものの、どちらも若かりし頃、完璧主義傾向が強く、神のイメージで苦しんでいた。一方は、キリストとの出会いによる神秘体験を祈りの体系へと昇華させ、もう一人は、教義（信仰義認）の確信へとつなげた。このコントラストも面白い。

　特にマンレサ時代は、持ち前の完璧主義的な傾向が、頭をもたげ、イニゴは、神経症気味になり、その特徴的な症状も自叙伝から読み取れる[36]。ある時期のマンレサで、イニゴは、現代で言えば、鬱的症状に苦しんで

36　A. GIDDENS, *Modernity and Self-Identity*, 1991, Cambridge参照。著者は、自らの理論を成長した人間において展開し、子どもだけではなく、成人した神経症患もその対象として含んでいる。

いたようである。自叙伝でも、「非常に味気ない気持ちになり、口禱の
ときもミサを拝聴する時も、その他の祈りの時も、少しも喜びが感じら
れなくなってしまった」（自叙伝21番）とあり、さらに「この間に幾度
も疑悩が起こって、ひどく悩まされた」（自叙伝22番）と書いている。
鬱は、自分に向けた怒りであるゆえ、マンレサでのイニゴは、過去に犯
した自分の罪に悩まされ、抑うつ的な気持ちに何度も陥っている。現代
の精神障害の診断・統計マニュアル（DSM-5）に照らし合わせてみても、
当時のイニゴには、少なくとも、抑うつ気分、集中力の低下、食欲減退、
気力の低下、決断困難、自尊心の低下、過剰な罪責感、そしてついには
自殺企図までもがあったことがわかる。自分の救いに関する妄想を伴っ
た不安など、彼の経験した危機は、霊的、心理的、そして生理的な内容
が含まれている。例えば、マンレサで、イニゴが、髪を伸ばし、手足の
爪も伸び放題にしていた。その時、彼が何を見たか、それは彼の心を悩
ませる幻想だった。やはり、この世にあるというのは、生きて、身体を
持っているということにほかならない。肉体的なものを軽んじ、極端な
節制や犠牲を課す生活は、彼のこころを荒みで満たしていった。それは、
生きることの緊張感を手放すことでしかなかった。生きることは、具体
的で、生理的なことである。食べることであり、身のまわりを気遣うこ
とであり、他者と交わることであり、内的・外的なある程度の緊張を生
きることである。

　カウンセリングやセラピーで大切な態度に、"Here and Now"「ここ
で、今」がある。この頃の若きイニゴの悩みは、「ここで、今」を生き
られなかったことによるものだとも考えられる。回心後の想像する眩し
いほどの自分の姿や偉業に心が囚われ、その姿と過去の自分のギャップ
に失望した。過去のあやまちに囚われ、自分でかき消そうとした。する
と焦りが増し、不安が彼を捕らえた。回心の基本は、Let go, let God で
ある。どのような状態であっても、神のいつくしみは、今、ここに生き
る人間とこの世界の中で陰に陽に注がれていることを信じることである。
身体性の重要さに触れたが、これも同じく、今、ここに、身体を持って

生きている自分を認める以外は、結局のところ、焦りや失望を生むほかないのである。

　その頃には、「今始まるこの全く新しい生き方は、一体何だろうか」（自叙伝21番）と少しずつ、客観的に自分を見つめることができるようにもなっていた。興味深いことには、彼が、徐々に自分を取り戻していく様は、なおざりにされた人間性を回復していくプロセスを通してのことだった。自叙伝には、詳しい回復の道筋は、書いていない。「かの霊動がどうやって起こってきたかを検討し、その結果、もう過去のことに関しては、今後一切告解しまいと決心した」（自叙伝25番）とある。今で言う、認知行動療法のような認識と取り組みの転換を行っている。そして、はじめて、身体を労る選択をする。「この照らしが善霊から来るのかどうかに疑いを抱き、ついにその照らしを捨て、定めた睡眠時間をとる方が良いという結論に達し、その通り実行した」（自叙伝26番）。自分の身体性を受け止めたこの選択は、実に大きな一歩だった。「主は、悪夢のようなものから彼を目覚めさせたのである」（自叙伝25番）とあり、霊的な変容があったことが暗示される。イニゴは、人々への同伴をはじめ、そこにやりがいを感じ始めると、いろいろの行き過ぎをやめ、身だしなみに気を遣うようになったとある。霊的な回心とはいえ、身体が下支えをしているのである。だからこそ、食べて、寝て、落ち着くという、当たり前のことが大切なのである。

　このマンレサで、自分の中に巣食う悪や闇と対峙する痛みや恐れを体験し、同時に差し出されるいつくしみ深い神の手も体験した。程なくして、カルドネル河畔で、照らしを体験する。自叙伝に「理性の目が開け始めた。（中略）これによって非常に明るく、照らされたので、全てが新しく感じられた」（自叙伝30番）とある。さらに、彼は、「理性に大いなる照らしを受けた」（自叙伝30番）と言っている。宗教的回心は、「こころ」と「魂」の領域だけではなく、理性（心理学的には、認知と言ってもいいであろう）にも変化が現れる。信仰と理性の両輪は、良い識別には不可欠なものである。これが、イグナチオの霊性の深みと独特な

ロジックとなって、後に『霊操』の基幹をなし、闇との対峙で、理性と情緒が混乱する人たちを光へと導く懐深い同伴の手立てとなる。イグナチオの霊性は、人間の抱える光と闇という現実に理解ある眼差しを持った霊性なのである。

　鬱と荒みについて簡単に言及する。荒みは、イグナチオ曰く、悪魔の仕業であり、単に落ち込みとか、苦しみというものではない。それは、霊的な原因ゆえに起こるものである。霊的成熟のための試みであり（霊操7番）、また敵が創造主から人間を引き離すためのものである（霊操317番）。鬱と霊的荒みが、重なることはあるが、本来、異なるものであることは、理解しておくべきであろう。それゆえに、重い鬱状態にある時は、霊操を控えるべきだと言われる。なぜなら、それは治療にならないどころか、悪化させる危険性があるからである。ただ、鬱状態にあっても、祈ることはできる。祈ることで大きな慰めを得、神の支えを感じることができる。実際、軽度の鬱症状の場合であれば、霊的同伴は、神に自分を開いていく効果的な機会となりうるのである。ここが、サイコスピリチュアルな着眼点である。

　私たちも、様々な形で、一時的に程度の差こそあれ、ある種の「落ち込み」を経験する。それは、もしかすると、自分の中で理想と現実のバランスが欠け、身体性が、なおざりになっているからかもしれない。また、無意識の世界に押し込めてしまっているモヤモヤとしたものを長く放っていることから来るかもしれない。そんな中で、収まりのつかない怒りや、不安、そして寂しさゆえに、バランスを欠いた行動に出てしまうことがある。ある意味、イニゴの陥った悪循環も、追い求める理想と現実の溝を埋められずに、行き過ぎた節制に身を費やしたことによるものだった。

　マンレサでイニゴは、こころの奥底でもう一度自分と出会い、この世のものでは癒せぬ渇きを感じた。こうして徐々にイニゴは、身体性を取り戻し、こころと魂の安定を取り戻した。こころの試練を通して、彼の理性は、より深い魂の領域に開かれていった。その時に、落ち着きを取

り戻し、歩み出した。巡礼者になるとは、歩くことであるから、実は本来、この身体性の回復と非常に関係が強いのである。イニゴは、彼独特の自己超越の道を少しずつ歩き始めた。回心には、Camino（道）という言葉が一番合う。迷うこともあれば、新たな道を見つけることもある。巡礼者としてのイニゴは、イグナチオ的霊性の原体験と言える。それは、歩み、時にとどまって、振り返り、さらに探し続けること。安寧をむさぼらずに、何かがあるのではと希望を胸に、もう一歩先（Magis）を求める態度である。ナルシシスティックな執着から解放されるに従い、マンレサの体験の後で、イニゴは、仲間を作った。何よりもともに歩く仲間の巡礼者を求めた。心身のバランスを保つためにも、また分かち合う喜びを得るためにも、仲間や共同体は不可欠である。試行錯誤の後、それがやっとパリ大学で実を結ぶのである。

　私たちは、起きてしまったことに対し、時間を巻き戻すことはできない。簡単ではないものの、その代わりに、そこに生きる力を見出し、そこから新しい認識や洞察を得ることはできる。現代の私たちも、イニゴのように何らかの傷や喪失体験を持っている。傷を抱えて生きるとは、傷つき、埋もれている自分の真の価値を、再び見出すということである。この世界では、ともすると知らず知らずのうちに、自我が肥大化し、見せかけの自分が一人歩きしてしまう。誇大化した妄想とも言える「こうあるべき」という意固地さではなく、変わることのできる自分のありようを認め、生きる意欲、可能性を見つけることが、自分の価値を見出すことである。「こうあるべき」自分から自由になって、「こうにもなれる」新しい自分に自信を持つのである。イニゴは、自身の身体の外傷と思い通りにいかない人生に直面し、人間存在の弱さと不完全さを嫌というほど味わった。しかし、それは、自身のレジリエンス（回復力）に気づく時でもあった。それも神によって引き挙げられるレジリエンスである。底をつく体験をしたが、神は彼を引き挙げ、彼の方もまた、新しく生きることを諦めなかった。

自己愛に支配されることに空虚さを覚え、自己の内奥から神への渇きを感じ、イニゴの感性と眼差しは、研ぎ澄まされ、奥行きと深みを得た。新しい自分は、生かされている自覚と感謝に満ちていた。イニゴは、自分で体験した、この祈りの奥深さを人々に伝えた。彼は、旅を続けながら、人々との交わりの中で、新しい霊的感覚（感性）を分かち合っていった。巡礼者として歩みを進めながら、神の存在を、そこかしこに見出す観想者となって、人々とのつながりを生きていった。それが、さらに新たな想像力と創造性を育み、この生き方を分かち合う仲間を形成していった。皮肉にも、大砲の一撃がなければ、イエズス会、すなわちイエスの仲間たちは生まれなかったであろう。このように、私たちも傷を抱えて生きるのは、痛みを伴うが、その上で、あらん限りの一歩を前に進めるレジリエンスも秘めているのである。また、それゆえに、他者への理解が育まれるのである。

　「すべてのものをキリストにおいて新しく見る」とはいったい何だろうか？　キリスト教の信徒が、全人口の2パーセントくらいしかいない日本で、キリストにおいて新しく見るという呼びかけは、正直ピンと来ないであろう。上智大学の学生たちにとってもそれは同じことである。キリストとは誰か、キリストとの人格的な出会い、キリストとの対話など、霊的生活の中心的なテーマとなりうる内容もキリストを知らない人々にとっては、あまりインパクトを持たない。ただ、イグナチオは、彼の回心体験から、霊的生活のプラクティカルな勧めを残してくれた。それが、「すべての中に神を見出す」である。だからこそ、先行する予備的な福音宣教が必要となるのである。「新しい眼」で見渡せば、世界はキリストという驚きに満ちている。しかし、それは、達観して見えることではない。イグナチオは、「キリストの人性を内的目で見たことがあった」（自叙伝29番）と言うように、その回心の道すがら、キリストという人格と出会うことができた。生きる意味を達観して生きている人は、誰もいない。生きながら、ある時ふと気がついたり、考えて、考え

尽くしてもわからなかったりと、様々である。イグナチオも、もしかしたら、老齢に差し掛かり、彼なりの生きて来た意味、生かされた意味を味わえるようになった時に、自叙伝を記す決意をしたのかもしれない。物わかりのいい、初めから聖なる人間ではなく、わからず屋で、迷い多き人間である自分。それでも、キリストに出会い、少しずつ新しく見る目を養いながら、神に生かされ、伴われ、必要とされ、遣わされた人生の語り部としての自分を受けとめることができたのであろう。

　イエズス会の伝統には、神による驚きの入り口へと続く、長く、ゆっくりと時間をかけた、人間的かつ霊的な旅路を同伴する伝統がある。私たちは、特に教育現場で働くキリスト者は、日ごろ接する青年たちに同伴し、分かち合う必要がある。キリストという驚きは、不完全な人間の持つ神秘性の中に潜んでいる。悲喜交々の日常や時として起きる不測の事態の中にあって、現代の若きイニゴたちに寄り添うことで、光と影を併せ持つ人間性の中にいるキリストの存在を探す手伝いをしていきたいものである。コロナ・パンデミックの今だからこそ、こころのケアのみならず、魂のケア（配慮）の必要性も、以前にも増して感じられる。若きイニゴたちが巡礼者となって、仲間を見つけて、自信と希望を胸に歩き続けられるようともに歩いていきたいものである。そのためには、まず私たちが、人間的かつ霊的遍歴の中、神の力に信頼して、歩む巡礼の仲間であることを自覚しよう。

　最後に、生前のイグナチオをよく知るナダル神父が残した言葉で、終わりたいと思う。

　「師父イグナチオは、聖霊と召命が自分を導くところに心を向け、深い謙虚さをもって聖霊に従い、聖霊より先に行こうとせず、己が人生を未知なる場所へと委ねた。この巡礼者は、イエス・キリストへの愛に駆られた愚か者のようだった。神が彼のこころのうちに入った瞬間から、彼は愛と奉仕の最良の方法を求めてヨーロッパ中を旅し始めた。彼の人生における情熱は、すべてのものの中に神を求め、見つけることだった」

Seeing All Things New in Christ

The Conversion of Ignatius of Loyola and its Significance
in our Contemporary World

Foreword

On May 20, 1521, Ignatius of Loyola (1491-1556), who was seriously injured at the siege of the fortress of Pamplona, underwent a spiritual experience that truly altered the course of his life, during his convalescence in his hometown at Loyola Castle and subsequent sojourn in Manresa. On the occasion of the 500th anniversary of the conversion of Ignatius, Superior General Arturo Sosa of the Society of Jesus issued a call to Jesuits around the world. The period extending from May 20, 2021 to July 31, 2022 was specified as the "Ignatian Year 2021-2022," and it was decided to reaffirm the mission of the current Society of Jesus from its origins, under the motto of "Ver nuevas todas las cosas en Cristo" / "To see all things new in Christ." (cf. Au 30,2)

At Sophia University, in response to this call concerning the Ignatian year, on October 9, 2021 the Sophia Symposium of 2021 was held by the university's Faculty of Theology with the full cooperation of the Jesuit Province of Japan, so as to ponder over events linked to the conversion of Ignatius and to study the present-day significance of the conversion. The event was co-sponsored by the university's Institute of Christian Culture and Catholic Jesuit Center, the topic being, "To See All Things New in Christ. The Conversion of Ignatius of Loyola (1521/1522) and its Significance in our Contemporary World."

At the symposium, the first address was delivered by José García de Castro Valdés, entitled "The Transformation of Ignatius of Loyola." Dr. García de Castro is a professor at the Faculty of Theology at the Pontifical Comillas University in the city of Madrid in Spain, and he happens to be a world-acknowledged authority on research linked to both Ignatius of Loyola as well as the spirituality of the Jesuits. He has abundant related works to his credit, and in his lecture he revealed that the conversion of Ignatius was primarily a process of gradual transformation.

In the next address, Dr. Yosuke Sakai delivered a lecture entitled, "The Conversion of Ignatius of Loyola and its Psycho-Spiritual Perspective." In September 2021, Dr. Sakai retired as lecturer in the Department of Psychology at the Pontifical Gregorian University in Rome, and he currently teaches at the Faculty of Theology and Graduate School of Applied Religious Studies, at Sophia University. Dr. Sakai conducts his enquiry from the angle of cooperation and integration of theology and psychology. In his lecture he tackled the conversion of Ignatius of Loyola from the standpoint of psycho-spirituality, integrating Christian spirituality and psychology.

Aside from Ignatius of Loyola who was the key protagonist in this symposium, the most vital and pivotal agent in his conversion, that transcendent and personal 'other' who kindled an innate shift in his life, was "God." The conversion of Ignatius was indeed an event that transpired between God and himself. While the existence of "God'" as a transcendent personal other, and the fact that a human life was altered by that "God," may not of necessity be issues known to all, yet the lives of the myriad individuals who followed the conversion of Ignatius over these past 500 years, serve as a stirring witness to the existence and work of "God," as the sublime and personal other.

This book is a compilation of the lectures delivered in this symposium. The lecture of Dr. García de Castro includes the original Spanish text as well as both Japanese and English translations, while the lecture of Dr. Sakai includes the original Japanese text and an English translation. Please note that aside from the translation of the lecture by Dr. García de Castro, all the English translations in this book are the work of Cyril Veliath, S.J., Professor Emeritus of Sophia University.

Who was Ignatius of Loyola?

● Hitoshi Kawanaka, S.J.

Ignatius of Loyola (1491-1556), whose name at birth was Iñigo López de Loyola, was born in 1491 in the Kingdom of Castilla to a family of provincial nobility in Guipúzcoa (in the present-day Basque country of Spain). He commenced his life as a page to a powerful nobleman, and led a glamorous court life while training to become a knight. At the beginning of his *Autobiography*[1], he looks back on those days and briefly remarks that "until the age of twenty-six he was a man given up to the vanities of the world, and his chief delight used to be in the exercise of arms, with a great and vain desire to gain honour." [Au 1,1]

In May 1521, an event arose that was to become the biggest milestone in his life. War broke out between Spain and France, and Ignatius was given command of the Spanish garrison at the Fortress of Pamplona, a front-line base against the French forces. The Spanish garrison at the citadel of Pamplona fought tenaciously, while they were being besieged by a vast French army. Nevertheless however on May 20, 1521, a French artillery shell happened to strike the leg of Ignatius, causing him to collapse with severe injuries. [Au 1,3] The Spanish garrison conse-

---

1   *El peregrino. Autobiografía de San Ignacio de Loyola*, Introducción, notas y comentario por JOSEP M.ª RAMBLA BLANCH, S.I., Bilbao-Santander: Mensajero-Sal Terrae, 1998 (3ª Edición).

quently decided to yield to the French, whereupon the French who were the enemies, paid homage to Ignatius for having courageously battled to the very end. Granting him the courtesy due to a knight they had him sent back to Loyola castle, to his hometown. On arriving at Loyola, Ignatius underwent several grueling surgeries without anesthesia, in order to set right his injured leg. However since the surgery proved ineffective and failed, one of his legs ended up being a bit shorter than the other. In the battle at the fortress of Pamplona, Ignatius had fought valiantly for his honor as a knight. Yet with just a single bullet, all that he had dreamed of and steadily built up as a future knight, was instantly destroyed.

While Ignatius was recuperating at his birthplace of Loyola Castle, he had nothing to do and lots of leisure. Hence he decided to read two books he happened to find in the Castle, and these were a biography of Christ that described his life, namely "The Life of Christ" (*Vita Christi*) by Ludolph of Saxony, and a biography elucidating the lives of Christian Saints, that is "Golden Legend" (*Legenda Aurea*) by Jacobus de Voragine. Having nothing else to read he picked up these books and began to read them, but while reading, he steadily developed an allure for the way of life pursued by Christ and the saints as presented in those books, and in due course there arose within him an aspiration to live like them as well. What this implied was to lead a life of service to others like Christ, and to dedicate one's life for the wellbeing of others. Thus the young Ignatius, who while pursuing glory as a knight had relinquished all hope of a bright future, nevertheless discovered an utterly new significance and purpose in life. This was the ideal of serving Christ as his new master rather than any secular individual, and to pursue a way of life that involved the offering of his services to Christ, through the service of others. [Au 17,3]

Ignatius, who had developed within himself both an intense veneration for the life of Christ and a yearning to live like him, decided to journey first to Jerusalem where Christ himself had lived, and follow in his footsteps.[Au 45,3] Accordingly, he departed from his hometown of Loyola and headed for Barcelona in order to sail to Jerusalem, but on the way to Barcelona he ended up making a long and unpredicted stay at the little town of Manresa. It was here that he underwent a spiritual experience that urged him to conduct a thorough re-examination of himself, and determine the direction of his life. The *Spiritual Exercises*[2] is a collection of methods of prayer, which Ignatius, on the basis of his own spiritual experiences, compiled in order to help others. [cf. Au 99,2]

In September 1523, after overcoming many hurdles, Ignatius was finally able to reach Jerusalem, the place of his dreams. Yet, as the Church authorities governing the city did not permit his residence in Jerusalem he was forced to return to Europe, and so on returning to Europe the first thing he did was to study. [Au 50,3] This was because he was acutely aware of the fact that to truly serve others, he had to remedy his lack of study and knowledge.

Ignatius thus embarked on study, and this was despite the fact that until then he had only received training as a knight. To pursue studies he consequently had to first master Latin, which at the time was vital for academic research, and so he duly commenced studying Latin by sitting beside school children much junior to himself. He later continued studies in various parts of Spain, starting with Barcelona and later Alcalá and Salamanca, but in every place he was viewed with doubt by the Church authorities. In 1528 Ignatius departed for Paris, which at the

---

2   IGNACIO DE LOYOLA, *Ejercicios Espirituales*, Introducción, texto, notas y vocabulario por CÁN-DIDO DE DALMASES SJ, Santander: Sal Terrae, 2021 (8.ª edición).

time was the center of academic research in Europe, and commenced studies at the University of Paris. He simultaneously persisted in his efforts to win over like-minded people who shared his ideals and aims, namely to serve Christ and serve others. His earlier efforts at finding comrades had been met with painful failures and setbacks, but during his study in Paris, he came across companions who would become the future founding members of the Society of Jesus.

During his study at the University of Paris, an individual who shared a room with Ignatius at the College of St. Barbara, which was a dormitory at the university, was Francis Xavier (1506-1552). Xavier, who hailed from an aristocratic family in the Kingdom of Navarre, was a proud, ambitious, and alluring young man with a passion for athletics, and initially he did not hide his rancor and disdain for Ignatius, with whom he shared a room within the dormitory. That was due to the fact that the shabby middle-aged student that Xavier noticed before him was the precise contrary of what Xavier himself aimed at, and so, far from welcoming Ignatius, he on the contrary even harbored feelings of animosity towards him. The backdrop to this reaction was the war between Spain and France, that had brought Ignatius to a pivotal turning point in his life. The head of the Xavier family was a vassal in the service of the Kingdom of Navarre, but when the Kingdom of Navarre sided with France, he was forced to fight against the Spanish army. With the defeat of France, the Castle of Xavier which had served as the abode of the Xavier family was utterly demolished by the Spanish army, leaving just a small living area for the family. This led to the collapse of the Xavier family. Burdened by such a ruthless past Xavier went abroad to study at the University of Paris, with the aim of enhancing his career. Although initially he was fervidly opposed to Ignatius, yet on interacting with him he in stages grew deeply entranced by his nature and way of life, and in time came to identify with his goals and ideals. He eventually became one of the most trusted companions of Ignatius.

Thus on August 15, 1534, the first seven companions including Ignatius took their vows in a small chapel in Montmartre, in Paris. These vows primarily involved poverty, chastity, and a journey to Jerusalem. These companions who took their vows at Montmartre served as the base of the future religious order, namely the Society of Jesus. Their vows at Montmartre included the clause that if for some reason their wish to travel to Jerusalem was not fulfilled after a period of one year, they would then proceed to His Holiness the Pope and seek his instructions regarding the matter. [cf. Au 85,2-5] Ignatius and his companions had already received the title of 'Magister' in March 1534, and in 1535, having completed seven years of study at the University of Paris, they set forth from the city. While in Italy they did make efforts to travel to Jerusalem, but an unforeseen conflict that arose between Venice and Turkey, put an end to all such dreams. Eventually however Ignatius and his companions abandoned plans of travelling to Jerusalem and proceeded to Rome instead to have an audience with His Holiness the Pope, and later on September 27, 1540, the Society of Jesus was founded by Pope Paul III, via the papal bull *Regimini Militantis Ecclesiae*. Since its founding in 1540 the Society developed rapidly and expanded its activities throughout Europe, and work related to education constituted the core of its religious activities. It was founded with the object of realizing the aims and ideals of Ignatius and his companions exclusively through educational activities, and it continues thus to this day, in the 21st century.

Ignatius of Loyola has often been compared to Martin Luther, and he has been viewed as a standard-bearer for the Counter-Reformation.

However, on observing the course of the life of the man Ignatius, or at least his "conversion" which was the starting point, there appears no sign whatever of any intentions with reference to the counter-reformation. Rather, on tracing the life of the man Ignatius what emerges clearly is the following of Christ, especially the poor Christ, and even the crucified Christ. For Ignatius, following Christ signified first of all "being like Christ (*como* Cristo)" (cf. Ex 93,2), that is, taking his way of life as our model, and living like him.

The central attitude of following the poor Christ has its basis on this. It is an affiliation between God and man based on Biblical faith, and it is overwhelmingly a work of God, which he has established with human beings. However, such a liaison does not mean that humans simply leave everything to God. On the basis of Biblical faith, the relationship established between God and man is a two-way relationship, between the prodigious work of God and humans who respond to it. Concerning this type of a Biblical bond between God and man, the Epistle to the Galatians 2:20 in the New Testament states, "It is no longer I who live, but Christ who lives in me." These words of Paul give us the impression of the work being done wholly through the power of the other. Nevertheless though, according to Biblical faith, a human being will never be like a robot programmed by God. It is only when each individual though his own free will responds to the awesome work of Christ, that a relationship between God and man is established. It is this two-way relationship between God and man, established via the overwhelming work of God, that Ignatius refers to as "with Christ" (*con* Cristo): "with me" (comigo) (Ex 93,3-4; 95,5). The existence of the Biblical God as a transcendent and personal other, and our response to his awesome power, are keys to understanding the true nature of Ignatius.

The Gospel of John 3:16-17, succinctly describes the significance and purpose of the entire event of Jesus Christ. "For God so loved the world that he gave his only Son, that whoever believes in him should not perish but have eternal life. For God sent the Son into the world, not to condemn the world, but that the world might be saved through him." The Christ event was solely for the salvation of people, and everything was directed for the sake of the people. So, the mission of Christ merely means aiding people, and creating a world wherein each human being is cherished as something irreplaceable. That indeed is the mission of the Church, which continues the salvific work of Christ.

Ignatius calls Christ's mission of building a better world, the "helping of souls" (ayudar a las ánimas). Here, the term "soul" (ánima) does not refer to a soul as a part of the human body. Rather, it refers to the total human being. Accordingly, what the term "helping of souls" signified for Ignatius was offering aid to people, and striving hard for them and for the creation of a better world. Judging by what we read in his *Autobiography*, it appears as though from an early stage after his conversion, Ignatius was aware of this helping of souls. For example, in number 45,3 of his *Autobiography*, the following is stated about him, directly after his conversion. "His firm intention was to remain in Jerusalem, forever visiting those holy places. And, as well as this matter of devotion, he also had the intention of helping of souls." Thus for Ignatius, following Christ clearly involved not just the choice of an individual way of life, but also the building up of a better world.

This mission of creating a better world, which is based on the events of Jesus Christ, is a universal human challenge wherein all people can share. Owing to the fact that it is a worldwide issue relevant to all mankind, it is possible for us to work in collaboration with all people, surpassing barriers such as religion and creed. After the Second Vatican Council, the current Roman Catholic Church affirms that this mission of Christ is never to boast of the superiority of Christianity over the non-Christian religions, or spread the impact of Christianity throughout the world. It is only when we approach the true figure of Ignatius who was moved solely by a desire to follow a poor Christ will we be able to attain a true vision of his face, as well as the faces of the Jesuits who looked up to him as their father and master. It is this desire and no other that constitutes the mission of Ignatius, as well as the mission of those who inherited his will.

La transformación de Ignacio de Loyola

José García de Castro Valdés, SJ

0 Introducción

En el tercer piso de la Santa Casa de Loyola (Azpeitia-España) hay una estancia que se conoce como la "capilla de la *conversión*". En esos, tal vez, 30 metros cuadrados se cree que estaba la habitación de Ignacio, donde pasó gran parte de los nueve meses que transcurrieron desde que llegó herido de Pamplona (mayo 1521) hasta que partió lleno de sueños y utopías hacia Jerusalén (finales de febrero 1522).

En esa capilla hay una frase escrita en la parte central del techo que dice: "Aquí se entregó a Dios Íñigo de Loyola". La tradición jesuítica ha venido identificando la experiencia de la *conversión* de Ignacio con ese proceso interno vivido durante su convalecencia y motivado principalmente por las lecturas piadosas que realizó (*Vita Christi* y *Flos Sanctorum*) y las mociones que estas desencadenaron.

Algo muy profundo debió de suceder en la interioridad de Ignacio para que en un tiempo relativamente corto produjera una transformación tan grande en el ámbito de sus deseos, de sus proyectos, de sus valores y también de sus sentimientos más profundos. Recordemos que Íñigo en 1521 era un hombre maduro (tal vez de 30 años), con una consolidada personalidad y profundamente enamorado de alguna dama de la corte cuya identidad todavía hoy desconocemos.

1 ¿Conversión o transformación / mutación?

Conversión es la palabra que ha pasado a la tradición ignaciana para referir, con mayor o menor acierto, a lo que aconteció en el interior de Íñigo López en Loyola ¿Qué pasó por el interior de nuestro protagonista a lo largo de estos nueve meses?

1.1. La conversión en los escritos ignacianos y en las primeras "vidas" de Ignacio de Loyola

Los primeros diccionarios de la lengua española (Covarrubias, 1611[1]) se refieren a la *conversión* como un elemento propio de la vida natural, "la mudanza de un ser en otro" y a la *conversión* del pecador como "la conversión de la Madalena" (Cov. s.v. Convertir[2]). "Significa también mudanza de vida: y regularmente de mala a buena" y ofrece el ejemplo de Santa Teresa en el cap. 9 de la *Vida*, donde leemos: "Era yo mui devota de la gloriosa Magdalena, y muchas veces pensaba en su *conversión,* en especial cuando comulgaba". (*Aut.* s.v. *Conversión*).

Aunque hemos de reconocer el cambio evidente y verificable de vida que se dio en Ignacio, observamos con curiosidad y cierta perplejidad que la palabra *conversión* no está presente en el vocabulario ignaciano. Ignacio no empleó *nunca* este término para referirse a un posible cambio de vida (ni en la *Autobiografía* [Au], ni en el *Diario espiritual,* ni en las *Constituciones,* ni en los *Ejercicios espirituales* [Ej][3]). En los *Ejerci-*

---

1   SEBASTIÁN DE COVARRUBIAS, *Tesoro de la lengua castellana o española,* Altafulla, Barcelona, s.v. Convertir.
2   El autor pone como ejemplo el cambio que experimenta el "agua cuando se convierte en carámbano o yelo".
3   I. ECHARTE (ed.), *Concordancia ignaciana,* Mensajero-Sal Terrae-Institute of Jesuit Sources, Bilbao-Santander-St. Louis 1996.

cios aparece una vez en la sección de los "Misterios de la vida de Cristo" para invitar al ejercitante a contemplar un verdadero caso de conversión, la "conversión de María Magdalena"[4]; no se menciona en la Primera semana, donde lo esperable podría ser provocar la *conversión* del ejercitante; pero no es esa la clave ignaciana.

La sorpresa aumenta algo más al comprobar que ninguno de sus primeros biógrafos utiliza este término en sus escritos oficiales para comentar este período de la vida de Ignacio en Loyola.

+ La primera biografía que tenemos, la del P. Diego Laínez (una larga carta escrita desde Bolonia julio 1547 al P. Polanco) tras aludir al proceso de agitación de diversos espíritus que Ignacio padecía durante su convalecencia, cierra este tiempo en Loyola de la siguiente manera:

> "*sin otro maestro exterior, ni comunicar su deliberación a otros,* **se determinó**, *con pretexto de ir a la corte del Duque de Nájera, de salirse de casa y* **totalmente** *renunciar a su tierra y a los suyos y a su mismo cuerpo y entrar en vía de penitencia*" [Ep. 4][5].

Laínez parece evitar la palabra *conversión* como hace también Juan Alfonso de Polanco, un año después en su *Sumario* de 1548, quien copia *literalmente* estas palabras de Laínez [*Sum* 11]. Pero, veinticinco años más tarde en la

+ *Vida de Ignacio de Loyola,* [1574] comenta:

> "**se propuso a sí mismo** *firmemente cambiar de vida y entregarse todo a Dios (aunque a ninguna persona se lo manifestó); pensó y* **determino** *de hacerlo realmente: marchar a Jerusalén, además del castigo de su cuerpo, la ab-*

---

4 "De la conversión de la Magdalena escribe san Lucas" [Ej 282]. Explicación de este misterio en F. RAMÍREZ, *El Evangelio según san Ignacio. La Vida de Cristo en los Ejercicios Espirituales y la tradición bíblica en la Vita Christi del Cartujano*, Mensajero-Sal Terrae-U.P. Comillas, Bilbao-Santander-Madrid 2021, 537-559.

5 A. ALBURQUERQUE (ed.), *Diego Laínez. Primer biógrafo de san Ignacio*, Mensajero-Sal Terrae, Bilbao-Santander 2005, 136.

negación de su honor y, en suma, toda humildad y aspereza. Al que deseaba agradar en gran manera a Dios, se le ocurría **emprender** *estos medios por su amor, pues no conocía otros mejores"* [*Vida* 9][6].

+ Por último, la obra considerada como definitiva acerca del fundador de la Compañía de Jesús, la *Vida de Ignacio de Loyola* de Pedro de Ribadeneira (1585), en su versión castellana, tampoco incluye la palabra *conversión*, aunque es el autor que con más detalle comenta aspectos "desordenados" del pasado de Ignacio:

> "diosse prisa y passó adelante, ayudándose por una parte de la lección [lectura]... y **trató muy de veras** consigo mismo de *mudar la vida y endereçar* la proa de sus pensamientos a otro puerto más cierto y seguro que hasta allí" [*Vida*, I, 2 [8]][7].

Estos primeros cuatro importantes testimonios de autores tan cercanos a Ignacio de Loyola parecen mostrar un cierto distanciamiento de la conversión a la hora de describir su experiencia. Verbos como "se determinó", "se propuso a sí mismo firmemente", "trato muy de veras" dan a entender que el cambio que se operó en Ignacio procedió más de un acto de su libre voluntad que de una irrupción espontánea de la gracia, como sería lo esperable al hablar de conversión.

1.2. Iconos bíblicos de conversión

María Magdalena o Pablo de Tarso son los personajes hacia los cuales miraba la tradición espiritual tardomedieval para comprender lo que era un caso de conversión: gracia recibida de lo alto, rasgos de alteridad, de iniciativa divina, cierta espontaneidad, cambio repentino de

---

6   J. A. DE POLANCO, *Vida de Ignacio de Loyola* (E. Alonso Romo, ed.), Mensajero-Sal Terrae-U.P. Comillas, Bilbao-Santander-Madrid 2021, 56-57.

7   P. DE RIBADENEIRA, *Vida de Ignacio de Loyola, Fontes Narrativi IV*, IHSI, Roma 1965, 91. Moderna versión inglesa: *The Life of Ignatius of Loyola* (C. Pavur, trans.) Institute of Jesuit Sources, St. Louis 2014.

vida…

No fue así como aconteció en Ignacio. Su proceso fue más lento, meditado, conscientemente asimilado donde el protagonismo evidente del "yo" fue constatando el trabajo silencioso de la gracia. La manera como aconteció el proceso interno de transformación en Ignacio fue diferente a como se entendía la conversión en la literatura espiritual de su época. Esta ponía el acento en una irrupción de Dios repentina e intensa en la vida de la persona, a la que reorientaba en su libertad sin poder, por otra parte, resistir o negarse a la propuesta del Espíritu. Veamos dos iconos del Nuevo Testamento.

a. La conversión de Pablo de Tarso

La idea y la experiencia de conversión en la mentalidad de Ignacio, de sus primeros compañeros y probablemente en el ambiente teológico espiritual de su época estaba más cercano a lo que puede acontecer en una elección de primer tiempo tal y como se describe en [Ej 175], que a lo que ocurrió a Ignacio, más o menos, en [Au 8-14].

Efectivamente, [Ej 175] describe el primer tiempo de elección; expone de manera muy breve cómo una persona puede reorientar su vida de manera cierta, consistente e indubitable desde una situación "de pecado" o contraria a los valores del Reino hasta convertirse en discípulo y apóstol comprometido con su Señor desde la primera línea del seguimiento de Cristo. Ignacio ilumina este párrafo [Ej 175] con las vocaciones de Pablo y Mateo. Pero esto NO fue lo que aconteció en Loyola.

Si por *conversión* se entiende lo que le pasó a Saulo de Tarso camino de Damasco es claro que no podemos entender como *conversión* lo que le pasó a Ignacio, porque por Ignacio y por Pablo pasaron por situaciones diferentes, tanto en sus causas (por qué), como en sus contenidos (qué) como en sus modos (cómo). El primer modo de elección [Ej 175] hace coincidir en un mismo instante de lucidez mística conversión, vocación y elección debido a una irrupción o entrada de Dios en la persona a la que alcanza en el fondo de su ser para conectar voluntad / afecto [experiencia] con entendimiento / razón [interpretación de la experiencia] y la libertad en acto [decisión historizada] y todo ello con una lucidez, convicción y certeza inapelables.

b. La conversión de María de Magdala

Otro icono bíblico de primera importancia para comprender lo que en tiempo de Ignacio se entendía por *conversión* es María Magdalena. Santa Teresa de Jesús se explica en estos términos: "Era yo mui devota de la gloriosa Magdalena, y muchas veces pensaba en su *conversión*, en especial quando comulgaba" (Santa Teresa, *Vida*, cap. 9). El *Tesoro* de Covarrubias incluye a esta mujer bíblica para ilustrar el significado de conversión: "Conversión del pecador, como la conversión de la Madalena"[8]. Ignacio, como vimos, vincula también directamente a la Magdalena con una experiencia de conversión [Ej 282], muy probablemente tomada de la *Vita Christi* I [60]: "De la conversión y penitencia de la Magdalena". Pero, de nuevo, lo que aconteció en Ignacio tampoco fue un encuentro con el Señor como refleja este pasaje del Evangelio.

1.3. *"Relectura" del proceso de Ignacio de Loyola*

Entonces, si propiamente los primeros testimonios no hablan de una conversión ¿qué le ocurrió a Ignacio de Loyola? Al evitar nombrar con la palabra *conversión* el proceso interno de Íñigo en Loyola (1521-22) los autores de la época (Laínez, Cámara, Polanco, Ribadeneira) nos están diciendo que lo que allí aconteció no fue una "conversión" en el

---

8 S. DE COVARRUBIAS, cit., s.v. *Convertir*.

sentido religioso habitual del término, sino una transformación interior de una persona hacia un seguimiento más radical del Señor, que fue evolucionando entre dudas, sombras, luces, aciertos y errores; una auténtica y cristiana transformación, sin duda, pero que no discurrió por los caminos de una habitual o estereotipada conversión, según los patrones propios del siglo XVI.

Por lo tanto, ¿en qué se diferencia la conversión representada en María Magdalena y en Pablo de Tarso de aquello que aconteció en Ignacio de Loyola? En tres puntos:

a. El estado vital y moral del que procede la persona. Ignacio no está situado en el ámbito moral del pecado como puede tratarse de un perseguidor de cristianos (Pablo) o una mujer pecadora (María).

b. En cómo acontece la relación con la gracia y la transformación del sujeto. Por iniciativa divina, directa e inmediata en María y en Pablo y en colaboración estrecha con la libertad y la determinación del sujeto en Ignacio.

c. En cómo interviene el tiempo en la experiencia de conversión o transformación: de manera inmediata en María Magdalena y Pablo y de manera ralentizada en Ignacio (9 meses).

Entonces ¿Cómo llamar a lo que aconteció en Loyola? No fue una conversión de un estado "A" a otro "B", sino una paulatina reorientación en la vida de una persona polarizada o atraída en su afecto, deseo y proyecto por un nuevo horizonte que poco a poco fue emergiendo en su vida y que tenía a Jesús de Nazaret como primer y poderoso centro atrayente de energía[9].

---

9   El P. García Mateo habló de *mutación*: "La gran mutación de Íñigo de Loyola a la luz del *Vita Christi* Cartujano". *Manresa*, 61 (1989), 31-44

La acción del Espíritu a través de la consolación y la implicación de la libertad de Ignacio a través de sus propósitos y determinaciones fueron tejiendo una decisión que no tuvo marcha atrás.

Llámese como se llame, hemos de reconocer que lo que aconteció en Loyola, fue una experiencia *"prínceps, primera, primordial"* que, por una parte, asumió la trayectoria anterior, de manera especial lo vivido por Ignacio en 1517, a sus 26 años y, por otra, ofreció un marco para la comprensión de aquello que Ignacio iba a vivir en los treinta y cinco años posteriores que le quedaban de vida[10].

Pero ¿de dónde venía esa experiencia? ¿en qué consistió? Y ¿hacia dónde apunta para su futuro inmediato? Porque no todo había comenzado en Loyola.

2 La transformación de Ignacio de Loyola

2.1. Fase 1. Profundidad y densidad de la vida. (Arévalo / Nájera 1517)

Si la batalla de Pamplona ocurrió en 1521 e Ignacio nació, como pensamos, en 1491, podemos concluir que en el momento en que cayó herido gravemente en Pamplona tenía *30 años*.

Luego la experiencia de comprensión de las vanidades del mundo, del ejercicio de las armas y del vano deseo de ganar honra a la que se re-

---

10 El traductor al euskera de la frase que se muestra en la capilla de la conversión acertó: no se conformó con escoger el caso "norengan" o "norengana" (en este caso: Jainkoarengan o Jaikoarenga-na) sino que hizo de ello un verbo: es el verbo de "orientarse" vitalmente no hacia un lugar o hacia una idea, sino hacia la persona de Dios (Jainkoarenganatu zen). Con este verbo, el sentido de ir en esta dirección aquí se superpone con el sentido de "permanecer", de estar, diríamos, polarizado. Hay, por tanto, una notable diferencia entre "entregar-se" y "quedar orientado/polarizado". Sobre todo, si pensamos en el peregrino y su movimiento y en que Dios en el primer caso se convierte en receptor (de una ofrenda), y en el segundo en el "imán" que atrae todas las cosas hacia sí.

fieren las primeras líneas de la *Autobiografía*, parece referirse a una experiencia cuatro años anterior, en 1517. ¿Qué pasó en la vida de Íñigo en 1517, cuando entonces, sí, tenía 26 años? Juan Velázquez de Cuéllar, contador Mayor del Reino, benefactor y protector de Ignacio, fue expulsado del palacio de Arévalo y con él debían abandonar la villa castellana todos sus sirvientes y adeptos, todo su "equipo", como diríamos hoy.

La expulsión de Arévalo marcó a Ignacio para siempre. La primera "bala de cañón" que había impactado con fuerza en su sólida personalidad no provenía de un soldado francés, sino de un fracaso castellano que venía a replantear su vida. Rumbo a Nájera, Íñigo experimentó una *nueva comprensión* de carácter filosófico y metafísico que, muy probablemente, le llevó a preguntarse por el sentido profundo de la vida, por el paso inexorable del tiempo, por la fugacidad del presente y la densidad de cada instante.

Dejando a sus espaldas todo un ambiente cortesano, superficial, un entorno de vanidades y apariencias, se sintió llamado a reorientar su vida para empezar a vivirla adulta y responsablemente. Tal vez se dio cuenta de que la vida no era un juego, sino que es algo que "va en serio"[11], como el tren que solo pasa una vez, una sola, única e irrepetible vez. Saliendo de Arévalo se daría cuenta de que antes o después hemos de entrar en el Misterio de la vida, si en verdad queremos comprender qué pueda significar esta tan simple como radical sentencia: "estoy vivo".

2.2. Fase 2. Vida y Misterio de Jesús de Nazaret (mayo 1521)

Esta primera comprensión puso los cimientos y capacitó a Ignacio

---

11 La comprensión primera de Ignacio tal vez pudiera verse poéticamente formulada cediéndole la palabra a Jaime Gil de Biedma: "que la vida iba en serio / uno lo empieza a comprender más tarde / como tantos jóvenes yo vine / a llevarme la vida por delante".

para recibir con generosidad y apertura esta *segunda comprensión* que le estaba esperando en Loyola cuatro años después. Si su primer aprendizaje por tierras riojanas (1517) le ayudó a entrar en lo profundidad de la vida, este segundo le conducía hacia la *Fuente* de la misma vida.

Si analizamos los testimonios de sus primeros compañeros (Laínez 1547, Polanco 1548, Cámara 1553, Ribadeneira 1585) constatamos que Íñigo experimentó un doble movimiento del corazón con respecto al mundo en que vivía, consolación y desolación[12]. Uno de los dos movimientos, la *consolación* tomó la iniciativa, y pronto se erigió en el responsable del proceso. Una vez iniciado, ambos caminaron de la mano; los dos movimientos se sucedían alternándose, y orientando los afectos en sentido contrario.

Algo tan simple, tan elemental e, incluso tan "pobre" como el mágico ejercicio de leer, aquello que hoy consideramos como el nivel más básico de cualquier formación (saber leer), se convirtió en el detonante de todo un proceso psíquico y espiritual que Íñigo no podía siquiera imaginar y tampoco supo controlar. En su casa de Loyola, dice la *Autobiografía* "no se halló ninguno de los libros que él solía leer, y así le dieron un *Vita Christi* y un libro de la vida de santos en romance" [Au 5].

No podemos dejar de valorar la importancia de la primera lectura en la conversión de Ignacio. Nunca agradeceremos suficientemente a Magdalena de Araoz, su cuñada, el gesto de haberle ofrecido unas piadosas lecturas "para pasar el tiempo" de su convalecencia.

El precioso texto de aquel monje cartujo, Ludolpho de Saxonia, que contaba las historias y anécdotas de Jesús y sus discípulos, cumplió su papel. Sus palabras y sus imágenes fueron cautivando poco a poco a Ig-

---

12 He intentado entrar con detalle en la transformación que Ignacio pudo haber vivido a partir de los escasos datos de que disponemos en J. GARCÍA DE CASTRO VALDÉS, "El proceso de simplificación de Ignacio", *El Dios emergente*, Mensajero-Sal Terrae, Bilbao-Santander 2001, 220-240.

nacio. Ignacio leía y leía (1) "por los cuales, leyendo muchas veces..." se aficionaba (2) a lo que hallaba escrito hasta que llega a afirmar: "*gustando mucho de aquellos libros*"(3) [Au 11].

Podemos imaginar a Ignacio, pasando las páginas de la *Vida de Cristo*, de un capítulo a otro, sin preocuparse demasiado por seguir un orden lógico. Una vez que cerraba los libros, cansado de leer, las historias de Jesús cobraban nueva vida en su imaginación y fantasía (4), después en sus sueños y deseos. Íñigo se vio envuelto en "pensamientos" sobre Galilea, apóstoles, bienaventuranzas, panes y peces, leprosos, ciegos y fariseos...

A través de la imaginación, Ignacio empezó a experimentar que un nuevo mundo, tan fascinante y desconocido, empezaba a emerger en su interior, y que discurría con libertad por los canales de su psiquismo y su emotividad; pero, sobre todo, lo más radicalmente nuevo y sorprendente eran las *repercusiones emotivas* (5) que todo eso empezaba a despertar en su interior.

Las historias de Jesús le llenaban de vida, encendían su ilusión y le regalaban una *alegría nueva* que tal vez nunca antes había sentido. Imaginar a Jesús y con Jesús era ya por sí mismo causa de vida y vida nueva. Era diferente de aquello que la vida cortesana le había venido proponiendo a lo largo de sus últimos 15 años y que después él llamaría "deleite" o "deleitación" [Au 1. 8; Ej 35]. Esta alegría era distinta.

Cuando quince años más tarde en Venecia, ya en 1536, estará dando los últimos retoques a su precioso libro los *Ejercicios espirituales*, escribirá en el párrafo 329:

"Propio es de Dios nuestro Señor y de sus ángeles en sus mociones dar *verdadera alegría* y gozo espiritual", es la primera regla de discernimiento de segunda semana. Ignacio no hablaba de una teoría aprendida en algún sermón de san Bernardo, en una conferencia de Juan

Casiano o en alguno de los tratados de Juan Gersón que tanto le influyeron. No. Ignacio hablaba desde su *experiencia*, de sentimientos y mociones que sólo pueden proceder de Dios. Dios, al darlos, suscita la alegría, comunica el gozo de su presencia. Era la primera vez que experimentaba algo así.

¿Dónde situar esta conversión? Si la primera experiencia de 1517 dejando Arévalo a sus espaldas, fue una conversión de contenido filosófico, existencial o metafísico, esta de Loyola iba descendiendo lenta pero imparablemente hacia la dimensión *religiosa* de su vida. ¿Cuál es la diferencia? La diferencia está en la aparición de la alteridad y la trascendencia como horizonte de sentido y Principio y fundamento de toda una vida. *Dios está aquí.*

Si en la conversión filosófica el sujeto se encuentra solo ante el la verdad de sí mismo y de su propia vida, que le anima a preguntarse "¿Qué hago o qué debo hacer para ser mejor persona?"; la conversión religiosa nos invita a preguntarnos: "¿Qué quieres de mí, Señor, para ser mejor seguidor tuyo, para estar más cerca de ti?".

Aunque desde niño había recibido una formación religiosa cristiana tradicional, ahora *religión* empezaba a significar otra cosa. Esta experiencia consistió en haber descubierto personal, experiencial y *consoladamente* a Jesús de Nazaret, Jesús en su humanidad, Jesús como Señor, como amigo, como compañero... Ignacio empezó a adentrarse en la dimensión vital y experiencial de la religión; empezó a "sentir y gustar" la alegría de estar con Jesús.

Pero la experiencia de Loyola no se conformó con haber desencadenado una atracción y fascinación afectiva por Jesús. Ignacio no se quedó paralizado en su admiración por su nuevo Señor y su Proyecto, sino que entró con ímpetu y energía en la dinámica de la imitación y del seguimiento de Cristo, sin más apoyos o metodologías que imitar a los apóstoles o a los santos de sus lecturas.

Ignacio decidió implicar su libertad de manera desproporcionada y todavía indiscreta, "esta ánima que aún estaba ciega" [Au 14]: "se propuso a sí mismo *firmemente* cambiar de vida y entregarse todo a Dios (aunque a ninguna persona se lo manifestó); pensó y *determino* de hacerlo *realmente*"[13] [*Vida* P. 9] y, en opinión de amigos y familiares, de manera indiscreta e imprudente [cf. Au 12].

Íñigo podría haberse quedado en Loyola y Azpeitia, colaborando activamente en el plan de pastoral de su parroquia[14]; podría haberse dedicado a animar la vida espiritual de las sencillas gentes del entorno o a organizar pequeñas estructuras de apoyo y solidaridad, obras de beneficencia para los más necesitados, tal vez algún tipo de ONG del siglo XVI.

Pero no. Íñigo interpretó que en este capítulo de su vida había que hacer algo grande por Cristo y puso su mirada en la mayor hazaña de las posibles: ni Montserrat, ni siquiera Santiago de Compostela ni Roma... buscaba ir a las fuentes primeras, allí donde todo había comenzado: "Jerusalén".

Por tanto, ¿A *qué* se convirtió Ignacio? La pregunta no es la correcta. En este momento de su vida es más adecuado preguntar: ¿A *quién* se convirtió Ignacio? Sobre todo, fue una conversión a una Persona, a Jesús, por la que sintió atracción, fascinación e imparable amistad. Una conversión no del todo diáfana, y sin duda, menos pura y acabada de lo que el mismo Íñigo creía... pero fue la experiencia *príceps* y primordial, suficiente y necesaria que posibilitó y dio consistencia, memoria y sentido a todo el proceso posterior.

---

13 Las palabras de Polanco recuerdan las de los Ej 98: "yo quiero y deseo y es mi determinación deliberada ...".
14 Parroquia de San Sebastián de Soreasu que sus padres regentaban y financiaban.

Esta incipiente amistad con Jesús, le fue llevando a ir tomando suave distancia de lo que hasta entonces había ido configurando *su* mundo. Dejarse atraer por Jesús, llevaba consigo tomar distancia de su vida pasada. Sin saberlo, estaba entrando en lo que el anónimo autor del clásico inglés del siglo XIV, *La Nube del no-saber*, ha llamado la nube del olvido: "ya se le iban *olvidando* los pensamientos pasados con estos santos deseos que tenía" [Au 10].

El Espíritu Santo había realizado gran parte del trabajo, tal vez el trabajo más difícil: des-afectarlo de la bandera de la vanagloria para atraerlo afectivamente hacia el nuevo ecosistema de la humildad que fluía de la cercanía con Jesús.

2.3. Fase 3. Reconfigurar el "yo" (Manresa 1521-Jerusalén 1523)

Encontramos a Ignacio convertido a la seriedad de la vida (1517), convertido a la amistad con Jesús y determinado a ir a Jerusalén.

Pero pecaríamos de ingenuos, de indiscretos y optimistas si afirmáramos que la experiencia de Loyola lo había logrado todo. Ignacio perdía de vista el Itzarraitz (el monte de Loyola) con la mirada clavada en el Tabor. Pero su transformación no era tan radical ni tan total como él mismo pensaba. Lo que *él creía* que se había convertido y lo que *de verdad* se había convertido coincidía en parte, pero distaba mucho de afectar al todo.

El proceso de la configuración con Cristo era una tarea más larga y también dolorosa de lo que podía imaginar. Soñar con Jerusalén, cambiar los vestidos o los zapatos, comprar un bastón de peregrino, dejarse crecer las uñas o los cabellos, o incluso reorientar su mundo afectivo-sexual no era suficiente para transformar una persona consolidada en un mundo interno de valores, deseos y aspiraciones mundanas. Su "yo", con ya 30 años de edad y una compleja estructura psicoemocional, era algo más duro de conquistar que la fortaleza de Pamplona.

Los once meses pasados en Manresa (marzo 1522-febrero 1523) le confrontaron con todo un mundo de desórdenes y tentaciones que el monje benedictino de Monserrat (Juan Chanones) supo acompañar con paciencia, sabiduría y prudencia.

Llama la atención comprobar cómo, en pocas semanas, Ignacio pasó de un optimismo y una euforia vital capaces de vencer todo obstáculo ante una de las empresas más "heroicas" de un peregrino (Jerusalén), a una pobreza y miseria radical, sumido en el sinsentido, tentado de suicidio y humillado hasta el punto de estar dispuesto a seguir a un perrillo vagabundo, si con eso pudiera recibir un poco de luz. "Muéstrame tú, Señor, dónde lo halle [alivio] que, aunque sea menester ir en pos de un perrillo para que me dé el remedio, yo lo haré" [Au 23].

a. La memoria de Jesús, la roca de la permanencia

Hoy nos llama también la atención que aquel hombre enamorado de Jesús, pero inmerso en una crisis tan profunda, no decidiera volver a Azpeitia. En medio de la noche, la memoria del pasado brillaría con intensidad. *¿Por qué no volver a casa?* El recuerdo de un hogar tranquilo y cristiano donde poder vivir también su relación con Jesús, emergería con fuerza. *¿Por qué no volver?*

La tentación se viste de sensatez y de buenos pensamientos: "Íñigo, vuelve a Loyola, administra propiedades, atiende los negocios de la familia; Íñigo, vuelve a Azpeitia, mejora la situación de tus paisanos, trabaja por los necesitados. Tu buena formación en Arévalo puede ser muy eficaz en Loyola. Íñigo, vuelve, puedes casarte, seguro que alguna mujer responsable y atractiva de Azpeitia, Bilbao o San Sebastián podría convertirse en una buena esposa; ...". Muchos pensamientos, todos buenos, muy humanos y sanamente religiosos.

Pero Íñigo no volvió, y este *no volver* nos habla también de la profundidad de su experiencia en Loyola. ¿Por qué Ignacio no abandonó su proyecto?

Tal vez porque se fió una y otra vez de la *consolación* que había sentido en Loyola; aquella *verdadera alegría* que sólo podía venir de Dios [Ej 329]. La experiencia de Loyola habitaba su memoria e Ignacio volvía a ella una y otra vez para descubrir en el pasado la luz para el presente y el sentido del futuro[15]. La experiencia de Jesús que Ignacio tuvo en Loyola fue la roca de los cimientos de su nueva vida; vinieron las aguas y la tormenta pero la casa resistió. Ignacio aguantó la prueba de la noche del sentido y la tentación del abandono. Era verdad, fue Verdad.

Ignacio no volvió porque confió en lo que había vivido; confió en sus propias fuerzas en las que reconocía la presencia de Dios. Confió en la fe en que Dios seguía ahí, aunque no lo sintiera como la consolación que había sentido en Loyola. El ego y el mal espíritu se lo pusieron difícil, muy difícil, pero la psicología de Íñigo aguantó la embestida.

b. El yo, combate más duro y persistente

Dice el Maestro Eckhart: "jamás hubo mayor virilidad, mayor guerra, ni mayor combate, que olvidarse de sí mismo y perderse"[16]. Esta era la batalla que ahora tenía que pelear Ignacio y que antes o después se le presenta a todo seguidor del Señor. Tal vez la más dura, la conversión del propio amor, del propio juicio... la conversión que exige entregar la vida y, sobre todo, entregar-se, a sí mismo. Era más fácil llegar a Jerusalén que al fondo de sí mismo.

---

15 Resuena la décima regla de primera semana [Ej 323]. La memoria de la consolación ofrece energía para atravesar la prueba de la desolación: "tomando nuevas fuerzas para entonces".
16 M. ECKHART, *El fruto de la nada*, Siruela, Madrid, 2001, 150.

b.1 Discernir la pobreza

Siguiendo el ejemplo de los santos, Íñigo confió de nuevo y se sumergió en la praxis de una pobreza actual, material; una pobreza visible, cuantificable, objetiva. Comida, bebida, ayuno, vestido, sueño y vigilias, disciplinas y penitencias... pero lo que en sí mismo puede ser interpretado como virtud objetiva, podía también actuar como impedimento camuflado para alcanzar la santidad pretendida.

Se veía un hombre vestido de saco, pero ¿qué había debajo de la áspera y ruda tela? Se veían unas sandalias pobres y rotas, pero ¿qué sostenía o, tal vez ocultaba, esta evidente descalcez?

Con el tiempo, Ignacio se dio cuenta de que esta pobreza tan visible y evidente necesitaba también ser discernida. Esta primera pobreza también contenía un componente "yoico" o egocéntrico que le podría estar alimentando un ego narcisista satisfecho por experimentar austeridades y sacrificios como tantos santos habían hecho.

Si no tenía cuidado, cito el texto, "esta ánima que aún estaba ciega... no mirando a cosa ninguna interior, ni sabiendo qué cosa era humildad, ni caridad, ni paciencia, ni discreción para reglar ni medir estas virtudes..." [Au 14], si no tenía cuidado, su propia relación con la pobreza podría ser interpretada como una conquista más en su *curriculum vitae* de victorias, nada más lejos de lo que, en verdad, pretendía, caminar con humildad con Jesús y hacia Jesús.

b.2 Su deseo, su camino, su propósito... ¿El camino de Dios?

Al referirse a Ignacio, la *Autobiografía* habla con frecuencia de *su* camino [Au 17], *su* costumbre, *sus* propósitos [Au 17], *su firme* propósito [Au 45], *sus* cuentas, *su* deseado vestido [Au 18]. Ya en Jerusalén el texto insiste: "*su* firme propósito [Au 17], *su* intención [Au 45], *su* buena intención [Au 46], *su* propósito, aquel que él no dejaría por ningún temor" [Au 45-46].

La inclusión en el texto de este repetido "su" es una deliberada y consciente opción del autor para ayudarnos a caer en la cuenta de que Ignacio está siendo llevado, todavía en gran medida por *su* propia voluntad y querer, siempre en proceso, en camino, en la tarea siempre pendiente de ir *venciéndose a sí mismo* para ir entrando (el gerundio es importante) en la rendición consolada a la Voluntad de Dios.

Buscando en todo responder a lo que Dios le iba pidiendo, Ignacio aprendió observándose minuciosamente a distinguir lo que más tarde escribirá en ese famoso párrafo [Ej 32] de los *Ejercicios*: "presupongo en mí tres pensamientos: uno que viene de mí mismo de mi mera libertad y querer y otros dos que vienen de fuera, uno del buen espíritu y otro del malo".

Desde el análisis de la experiencia, Ignacio fue aprendiendo a separar aquello que procedía de *su* propio deseo, querer y voluntad de lo que procedía del deseo o de la voluntad de Dios.

Es el aprendizaje que apunta hacia la desposesión, hacia la rendición y dicho también más dramáticamente, hacia nuestra propia muerte. Es el aprendizaje de tomar cada día la cruz que garantiza que no cargamos solo con nuestros deseos, nuestras intenciones o proyectos por muy evangélicos o buenos que sean o que puedan parecernos, sino que vivimos entregados a asumir con fe el deseo, la voluntad, el proyecto y la acción de Dios en nosotros. Nuestra vida no es tan nuestra como pensamos; es antes y sobre todo, *Su* Vida, vida suya en nosotros.

Esta conversión del yo, del "sí mismo" no tiene fin, se trata de una experiencia de carácter asintótico. Como nuestro Señor hizo con Pedro, estamos abiertos a que Jesús en cualquier momento nos llame a parte y nos pregunte repetidamente acerca del amor: "Íñigo, ¿me quieres?" (Jn 21). Mucho más importante que mis propias y devotas hazañas por

Cristo es descentrarse del ego y permanecer voluntaria y decididamente en su amor, con o sin hazañas, esto es secundario.

2.4. Fase 4. El deseo y la voluntad de la Iglesia (Jerusalén, 1523) [Au 45-48].

Esta tercera conversión, a la dimensión más *antropológico-teológica y esencial de la pobreza* adquirió una nueva luz, repentina e inesperada, a finales de setiembre de 1523. El Provincial de los franciscanos, custodios de los santos lugares, amenazó a Ignacio con la excomunión si no abandonaba en los plazos convenidos Jerusalén y regresaba a su lugar de partida. Mucho más que una anécdota histórica, sin duda desagradable para las dos partes, se trató de un nuevo impacto, como si otro nuevo "cañonazo" golpeara a Ignacio y viniera a dejar, otra vez, inválida la orientación de su nueva vida.

Ignacio había invertido dos años duros en llegar a Jerusalén con *su firme propósito* [Au 45.46] de permanecer allí; ahora, tras solo veinte días de visita cultural y espiritual, había de regresar a su tierra sin posibilidad de discusión ni diálogo.

Es interesante comprobar que es, precisamente, tras esta nueva crisis en Jerusalén cuando aparece por ¡primera vez! en la *Autobiografía* la expresión "voluntad de Dios"; cito: "después que el dicho peregrino entendió que era *voluntad de Dios* que no estuviese en Jerusalén" [Au 50].

Con la autoridad eclesial, irrumpe con evidencia y energía una nueva variable en el proceso de conversión de Ignacio. Hasta ahora, la experiencia religiosa tenía dos protagonistas: Ignacio y Jesús, y estos se encontraban en la interioridad / subjetividad del peregrino, en una relación estrecha, íntima y afectiva.

Pero ahora Ignacio tiene que abrir su experiencia a un tercer elemento, fuente de autoridad no sólo jurídica, sino también teológica y mística. Pero esto Ignacio no lo entiende. En 1523 le bastaba con obedecer para salir del paso e integrar en su momento histórico lo que el provincial franciscano le indicaba. En medio de su desconcierto y su nuevo fracaso, aceptó el vínculo *Iglesia – obediencia – voluntad de Dios*, pero todavía tardaría en comprender internamente la mística que inspiraba y fundamentaba esta trilogía.

Lo que él creía hasta ahora, como criterio único y suficiente: los movimientos (mociones) discernidos de su interioridad, para acertar en su particular seguimiento de Cristo, viene a verse redimensionado por una instancia superior que pide paso urgente en sus procesos de discernimiento.

El sólido carácter *yoico* de su proceder se seguía abriendo a nuevos modos de comprender la relación con Dios, en este caso a lo que más tarde formulará como "nuestra santa madre Iglesia hierárchica" [Ej 353].

Esta crisis de Jerusalén nos abre el paso a nuestro siguiente punto. El Espíritu dosificaba los elementos de la conversión según aquello de *Eclesiastés*: "hay un momento para todo y un tiempo para cada cosa bajo el sol" (Ecl 3,1).

2.5. Fase 5. Mirada del otro, Rostro de Dios (Barcelona 1523-Paris 1534)

Parece que Ignacio entró en Jerusalén el 4 de setiembre de 1523 y salió de la ciudad Santa rumbo a Jafa, para regresar a Venecia, el 23. Apenas veinte días habían sido suficientes para desvanecer el sueño en el que había invertido tantas esperanzas y energías. ¿Qué pasó en Jerusalén y qué puede tener que ver este breve lapso de tiempo con la exploración que estamos haciendo sobre la conversión de Ignacio?

No tenemos mucha información sobre el paso de Ignacio por Jerusalén. La *Autobiografía* nos sorprende de nuevo y dedica tan sólo cuatro párrafos a este episodio de Ignacio por los lugares santos [Au 45-48] y de ellos, resulta que los tres últimos (¡) están dedicados a explicar los conflictos con su salida. Ignacio es muy parco al hablar de su experiencia interna: "la misma devoción sintió siempre en las visitaciones de los lugares santos" [Au 45][17].

Para adentrarnos en esta quinta *comprensión* / conversión hemos de retrotraernos de nuevo a Loyola y acercarnos a otro de "sus" propósitos, a otra de aquellas iniciativas que Ignacio asumió desde el comienzo sin pararse a pensar demasiado si aquello era o no era voluntad de Dios.

Al abandonar su casa paterna, Íñigo estaba convencido de que Dios le llamaba a una empresa solitaria, a reorientar y recomenzar su vida en soledad y a vivir su recién descubierta vocación en una relación de exclusividad con su nuevo Señor, con Jesús.

La *Autobiografía* nos lo permite concluir: en cuanto pudo, "dejó a su hermano en Oñate" [Au 12] y poco más adelante "despidiendo [en Navarrete] a los dos criados que iban con él" [Au 13] siguió su camino hacia Montserrat; "se partió *solo* en su mula", y más adelante, cuando ya desde Barcelona va camino de Venecia, "aunque se le ofrecían algunas compañías, no quiso ir sino *solo*" [Au 35] y el mismo Ignacio parece explicar por qué:

"porque él deseaba tener tres virtudes: caridad y fe y esperanza; y llevando un compañero, cuando tuviese hambre esperaría ayuda de él; y cuando cayese, le ayudaría a levantar; y así también se confiaría dél y le ternía afición por estos respectos; y que esta confianza y afición y esperanza la quería tener en un *solo Dios* [...] tenía deseos de embarcarse, no

---

17 Algo más sabemos por Polanco: "se llenaba de tanto gusto y sentimiento de consuelo espiritual, que lo que primero que había pensado, entonces con mucha más certeza lo determinó, a saber, permanecer allí" (*Vita*, 82 [30], único párrafo que dedica a la estancia de Ignacio en Tierra Santa).

solamente *solo*, mas sin ninguna provisión" [Au 35].

Ahora bien, ¿hasta cuándo perdura en Ignacio este deseo, *su* deseo, de construir *su* vocación en soledad? A mi modo de ver, muy probablemente, Ignacio replanteó este aspecto de su vida durante el viaje de vuelta de Jerusalén. Conociendo a Ignacio, es muy probable que desde el 3 de octubre que sale de Jafa hasta mediados de enero de 1524 que llega a Venecia (algo más de tres meses), nuestro peregrino estuviera recordando y orando, "sintiendo y gustando internamente" todo lo que había visto y experimentado en Tierra Santa.

Y al recordar... Ignacio entendió que caminar por los mismos lugares de Jesús llevaba el implícito de andar por los mismos lugares de sus discípulos. Ignacio comprendió que Jesús rara vez caminaba solo y que, por tanto, ser contado entre los amigos y discípulos de Jesús implicaba empezar a formar parte de una comunidad, de un grupo.

Pensar en Jesús y desear ser parte de sus amigos pasaba necesariamente por ser reconocido como miembro de un grupo, un grupo de amigos, de sus discípulos, de compañeros. Aunque no podía ni debía renunciar a la relación personal y original que iba construyendo con su Maestro, empezó a comprender la dimensión social del seguimiento, su estructura colegiada, societaria, su carácter *eclesial*.

Sí, muy probablemente fue a partir de su experiencia en Tierra Santa cuando Ignacio *repensó* y comprendió su nueva manera y estilo de estar con Jesús. Tal vez se sintió resituado en un modo de seguimiento menos centrado en sí mismo y más como parte de un grupo de seguidores, de una pequeña iglesia que él acabaría llamando "Societas Iesu", "mínima Compañía de Jesús".

Por eso, aunque tan breve, la experiencia de Jerusalén fue clave en este aspecto y marca un antes y un después en la manera de Ignacio de comprender y comprender-*se* en el discipulado. Había de encontrar compañeros. De nuevo en Barcelona (1524) y gracias a la generosidad de su buena amiga Isabel Roser, pudo adquirir el nivel de latín necesario como para poder ser admitido en la universidad de Alcalá y poder iniciar estudios "para ayudar a las almas"; pero el tiempo en la ciudad de la Catedral del Mar [Barcelona], fue también el comienzo de la las primeras tentativas por consolidar un grupo de compañeros.

Barcelona, Alcalá y Salamanca ofrecen no poca información de las peripecias que Íñigo vivió con Calisto de Sá, Diego de Cáceres, Juan de Arteaga y Juan Reynalde, a quien llamaban Joanico. Juntos vivieron episodios propios de estudiantes universitarios, las primeras adaptaciones de los ejercicios espirituales y otras aventuras un poco más duras con las autoridades de la Inquisición. Nos consta que fueron buenos amigos y se quisieron. Ignacio compartió la celda de Salamanca con Cáceres en situación verdaderamente incómoda y todos juntos programaron una nueva etapa de sus vidas en Paris, pero el sueño nunca se vio realizado. "Determinado de ir para París, concertóse con ellos que ellos esperasen por allí [Castilla] y que él iría para poder ver si podría hallar modo para que ellos pudiesen estudiar" [Au 71].

Es de todos conocidos que este primer grupo de compañeros no salió adelante; pese a que Ignacio les escribía con frecuencia [Au 80] desde la ciudad del Sena, ninguno viajó a París. "Calixto se fue a la corte de Portugal y de ahí a las Indias" de donde regresó rico; Cáceres volvió a Segovia, que era su patria" y Arteaga murió "en extraño accidente" habiendo sido nombrado obispo en México.

Pero la conversión de Ignacio al grupo era otro punto de no retorno. Quería continuar su seguimiento de Cristo con otros compañeros y así, tras un pequeño tiempo de búsqueda en París, vino a coincidir en el colegio de Santa Bárbara con un saboyano y un navarro, Pedro Fabro y Francisco de Jasso, de Javier, que como es bien sabido formaron el primer núcleo de lo que doce años después de la entrada de Ignacio en la Sorbona sería la Compañía de Jesús.

Tras Fabro y Javier, otros cuatro compañeros vendrían a sumarse al grupo. Diego Laínez, Alfonso Salmerón, Nicolás de Bobadilla y Simón Rodrigues. No es el momento ni el lugar para detenerse en la vida de este grupo ni analizar las claves internas de su funcionamiento, ni para compararlo con el grupo primero de Alcalá. Ahora nos basta afirmar que al proceso de conversión de Ignacio venía a sumarse esta nueva pieza que lenta y silenciosa, pero armónicamente, junto con todas las demás, iban configurando un carisma nuevo en la Iglesia.

Este grupo llegó a sellar su compromiso de permanecer juntos después de los estudios en la liturgia de la capilla de san Dionisio, en Montmartre, a las afuera de París y prometieron viajar *juntos* a Jerusalén si las circunstancias se lo permitían. Aquel 15 de agosto de 1534 ninguno de ellos podía imaginar que 6 años después estarían delante del papa Paulo III pidiéndole que les reconociera como un *grupo* nuevo en la Iglesia, una nueva orden religiosa (¡una más!) y que iban a ser enviados como misioneros del papa por lugares insospechados.

Tal vez al abandonar París a principios de abril de 1535, camino de su Azpeitia natal, otra despedida más, Ignacio pudo recordar la fecundidad de lo que doce años antes había vivido como doloroso fracaso en Jerusalén. En la mula que sus compañeros le habían alquilado, podía recordar su salida forzosa y contra su voluntad de Tierra Santa, como obra de una providencia escondida que iba guiando un itinerario que ya no le pertenecía.

Desde la distancia geográfica y temporal, aquel provincial franciscano, el P. Marcos de Salodio, aparecía para Ignacio como parte de un diseño de Dios que no dejaba de sorprenderle.

El fracaso y la muerte de *su* firme propósito de quedar en Jerusalén resucitaba en una fecunda etapa de estudios en París y, sobre todo, en un grupo de *"amigos en el Señor"* que había entrado en su vida y en su historia para quedarse definitivamente.

2.6. Fase 6. *"La conversión al mundo y a sus cosas"*

He dejado para el final de este proceso, la conversión llamada "al mundo y a sus cosas" porque me parece que, tanto en el proceso espiritual y místico de Ignacio como en su propuesta sistemática en los *Ejercicios espirituales,* constituye el puerto de destino hacia el que desea orientar a toda persona que se reconozca discípula del Señor desde esta perspectiva ignaciana.

Como en las conversiones anteriores en las que Ignacio fue reorientando su vida hacia la densidad del vivir, hacia la amistad con Jesús, hacia la pobreza del corazón o hacia el otro como mediación del *Otro*, también experimentó un giro profundo y sin retorno hacia el mundo y sus cosas. ¿En qué consistió esta conversión?

El punto de partida. Tal vez inspirado por el ejemplo de algunos de los santos, Ignacio sintió en los comienzos una inclinación a una salida del mundo, a un retiro vital… algo en él parecía sugerirle con insistencia abandonar el mundo, "sacarlo del mundo"; deseaba ser parte de esa corriente espiritual *"fuga mundi"* que animaba a encontrar el sentido verdadero de la vida, la paz y con todo ello a Dios, en el silencio de alguna clausura religiosa o de alguna cueva alejada de todo atisbo de bullicio secular.

Volvamos a nuestro texto. En la *Autobiografía* leemos: "Y echando sus cuentas de qué es lo que haría después que viniese de Jerusalén ofrecíasele meterse en la Cartuja de Sevilla, sin decir quién era para que en menos le tuviesen" [Au 12]. Pese a que desde Loyola enviaron a un empleado de hogar para que se informase bien de la regla de la Cartuja de

Miraflores de Burgos, "y la información que della tuvo le pareció bien" [Au 12], esta opción que todavía veía como posibilidad lejana, no le preocupó más.

Lo que sí le ocupó tiempo y espacio interior fue la búsqueda de soledad, hasta el punto de pretender construir un proyecto de vida personal tan ingenuamente fiado de Dios que pudiera prescindir de todo contacto con las estructuras y medios humanos de proceder: Familiarizado con las cuentas y presupuestos de palacio, Ignacio se pasó al otro extremo y evitaba todo posible contacto con el dinero; acostumbrado a vivir en la abundancia, prefería ahora vivir en el hoy sin proveerse para el mañana; acostumbrado a tener sus parcelas de fama y reconocimiento (sus seguidores en Instagram o Twitter, diríamos hoy), prefería ahora dejarse llevar por el deseo sincero de pasar desapercibido como modo de retirarse de escenarios públicos demasiado conocidos para él.

Esa etapa de devoto anacoreta en Manresa fue necesaria para su proceso personal, pero pronto comprendió que sólo constituía una estación más en el camino y que el Espíritu tiraba de él hacia otros horizontes de sentido más allá de penitencias y austeridades desmedidas... e indiscretas.

¿Cómo se operó esta transformación? ¿Cómo entender esta transformación del deseo incial de huida del mundo a una institución, la Compañía de Jesús, volcada al mundo y a sus cosas? Todo comenzó en un devoto paseo siguiendo la orilla de un río tal vez en agosto de 1522.

Poco sabemos de aquella experiencia conocida como "ilustración del Cardoner". Como experiencia cognitiva e intelectual, Ignacio tuvo una intuición metafísico-mística en la que entendió que "todas las cosas le parecían nuevas" [Au 30]. Podríamos preguntar a Ignacio en qué pudo haber consistido esta "novedad" y qué vio aquella tarde en *las cosas* que antes no había visto.

En fecha tan temprana, pocos meses después de haber salido de Loyola, Ignacio no alcanzó a comprender lo que le aconteció mientras estaba sentado cara al río, aunque fue una de las experiencias que más intensamente marcó su vida y que recordaría como primigenia e inspiradora treinta años después en Roma.

A mi modo de ver, esta experiencia del Cardoner puso el fundamento histórico-místico a uno de los elementos centrales y estructurales del carisma ignaciano-jesuítico: su opción constitutiva por el mundo, sus cosas y sus gentes; la opción por la historia y el tiempo y lo que en ellos acontece, sobre todo a sus habitantes.

Con el paso de los años, Ignacio fue girando en su manera de interpretar *el mundo*, pasando así de una primera mirada de desconfianza, recelo o incluso de cierto miedo, hasta incluirlo como elemento irrenunciable de su experiencia espiritual. Seguir a Jesús incluye *trans-portar* el mundo con uno mismo, asumirlo como parcela pneumatológica de mi responsabilidad cristiana. El mundo y sus cosas y su diversidad de personas... son siempre algo nuevo. "que todas las cosas le parecían nuevas" [Au 30, Cardoner] y esta novedad consiste en el fundamento amoroso y divino que todo lo habita y todo lo sostiene.

Ignacio fue elaborando, poco a poco, una teología espiritual implícita acerca de esta religación del mundo con su Creador o esta vinculación de la Divinidad con la Mundaneidad. Dios mira al mundo y mirándolo lo quiere y su querer todo lo habita y lo resignifica.

Para un más profundo conocimiento de lo que venimos diciendo, ahora sólo podemos apuntar muy brevemente dos claves. La primera nos la ofrece el segundo miembro de la primera parte de la definición de consolación que Ignacio ofrece en el párrafo 316 de los *Ejercicios*: "llamo consolación..." Ignacio añade: "y *consecuenter* cuando *ninguna* cosa criada sobre la *haz de la tierra* puede amar en sí sino en el Criador de todas ellas".

Para Ignacio, experimentar la consolación como experiencia inmediata del amor de Dios conlleva una *remitencia* también tan necesaria como inmediata hacia el mundo y sus cosas. Haber sido alcanzados *así* por el amor de Dios implica vincularse amorosamente con el mundo y sus cosas, *todas* sus cosas (ninguna cosa criada... la haz de la tierra), porque, desde la clave de la consolación, se nos ofrecen en su última identidad, en lo que verdad son, criaturas como yo habitadas por el mismo amor que a mí me sostiene y fundamenta.

La otra clave que justifica este giro hacia el mundo y sus cosas, como no podía ser de otra manera, la encontramos en la contemplación para alcanzar amor que cierra los *Ejercicios espirituales* [Ej 230-237]. Dios habita, trabaja y labora en este mundo. Este es el punto de llegada. Desde aquella primera conversión a la vida en 1517, Ignacio ha ido integrando dos realidades fundamentales: Dios y Mundo. Lejos de presentarse como dos componentes de una dialéctica irreconciliable, su propia relación con Jesús le ha ido llevando suavemente a adentrarse en la dimensión *creatural* del mundo para implicar "todo su haber y su poseer" [Ej 234] en su progresiva dignificación de la historia. Así, la misión que nace de la amistad con Jesús (Rey Eternal [Ej 98]) se dirige al Mundo, donde el mismo Dios está esperando, llenándolo todo con su Espíritu.

Conclusión. 5 puntos para "reflectir y sacar provecho"

+ La experiencia de Ignacio nos muestra que Dios y el hombre tienen, a veces, hermenéuticas diferentes: lo que para el ser humano puede ser leído como un fracaso radical (herida), para Dios puede ser el comienzo de una nueva vida llena de Sentido.

+ La conversión de Ignacio nos llena de optimismo al hacernos ver que la energía de la gracia es siempre mayor que las resistencias que nosotros ponemos al Espíritu.

+ La conversión de Ignacio nos anima a mirarnos en continua construcción, en proceso edificado silenciosamente por el Espíritu cuya lógica en ocasiones no alcanzamos a descubrir, pero que se va desvelando retrospectivamente, descubriéndonos así la mistagogía amorosa e irrepetible de Dios con cada uno.

+ La conversión de Ignacio nos invita a mirarnos con paciencia y misericordia y nos ayuda a entrar en el tiempo y en los procesos de Dios, cuyo Reloj, tantas veces, avanza a ritmo diferente al nuestro.

+ La conversión de Ignacio, en definitiva, nos anima a vivir desde la *consolación* como la Palabra pronunciada por Jesús en lo profundo del corazón, la única Palabra que permanece como un Eco en la crisis del sentido, como una Luz de la memoria en la noche de la Fe.

The Transformation of Ignatius of Loyola

○ José García de Castro Valdés, S.J.

0 Introduction

On the third floor of the Santa Casa de Loyola (Azpeitia-Spain) there is a place known as the "*conversion* chapel". In those, perhaps, 30 square meters it is believed that Ignatius' room was there, where he spent a great part of the nine months that elapsed since he arrived wounded from Pamplona (May 1521) until he left full of dreams and utopias towards Jerusalem (end of February 1522).

In that chapel there is a phrase written in the central part of the ceiling that says: "Here Íñigo de Loyola surrendered to God". The Jesuit tradition has been identifying the conversion experience of Ignatius with that internal process lived during his convalescence and motivated mainly by the pious readings he made (*Vita Christi* and *Flos Sanctorum*) and the motions they triggered.

Something very profound must have happened in the interiority of Ignatius so that in a relatively short time he produced such a great transformation in the sphere of his desires, his projects, his values and also his deepest feelings. Let us remember that Íñigo in 1521 was a mature man (perhaps 30 years old), with a consolidated personality and deeply in love with some lady of the court whose identity we still do not know today.

1 Conversion or Transformation / Mutation?

Conversion is the word that has passed into the Ignatian tradition to refer with, greater or lesser success, to what happened in the interior of Íñigo López at Loyola.

1.1. Conversion in the Ignatian writings and in the early "Lives" of Ignatius of Loyola

The first dictionaries of the Spanish language (Covarrubias, 1611[1]) refer to *conversion* as an element proper to natural life, "the change of one being into another" and to the *conversion* of the sinner as "the conversion of the Magdalene" (Cov. s.v. Convertir[2]). "It also means change of life: and regularly from bad to good" and offers the example of St. Teresa in chapter 9 of the Life, where we read: "I was very devoted to the glorious Magdalene, and I often thought of her conversion, especially when she received communion" (*Aut.* s.v. *Conversion*).

Although we must recognize the evident and verifiable change of life that took place in Ignatius, we observe with curiosity and certain perplexity that the word *conversion* is not present in the Ignatian vocabulary. Ignatius never used this term to refer to a possible change of life (neither in the *Autobiography* [Au] , nor in the *Spiritual Diary*, nor in the *Constitutions*, nor in the *Spiritual Exercises* [Ex][3]). In the *Exercises* it appears once in the section on the "Mysteries of the life of Christ" to in-

---

1 SEBASTIÁN DE COVARRUBIAS, *Tesoro de la lengua castellana o española*, Altafulla, Barcelona, s.v. Convertir.
2 The author gives as an example the change that "water undergoes when it becomes icicle or yelo".
3 I. ECHARTE (ed.), *Concordancia ignaciana*, Mensajero-Sal Terrae-Institute of Jesuit Sources, Bilbao-Santander-St. Louis 1996.

vite the retreatant to contemplate a true case of conversion, the "conversion of Mary Magdalene "[4]; it is not mentioned in the First Week, where it might be expected to provoke the *conversion* of the retreatant; but this is not the Ignatian key.

The surprise increases somewhat when we see that none of his early biographers use this term in their official writings to comment on this period of Ignatius' life in Loyola.

+ The first biography we have, that of Fr. Diego Laínez (a long letter written from Bologna July 1547 to Fr. Polanco) after alluding to the process of agitation of various spirits that Ignatius suffered during his convalescence, closes this time in Loyola in the following way:

"without another external master, nor communicating his deliberation to others, he **determined**, under the pretext of going to the court of the Duke of Nájera, to leave home and **totally** renounce his land and his own and his own body and to enter into the way of penance" [Ep. 4][5].

Laínez seems to avoid the word *conversion* as does Juan Alfonso de Polanco, a year later in his *Sumario* of 1548, who copies literally these words of Laínez [Sum 11]. But, twenty-five years later in his

+ *Life of Ignatius of Loyola*, [1574] he comments:

"he **firmly proposed** to himself to change his life and to surrender everything to God (although to no person he manifested it); he thought and **determined** to really do it: to march to Jerusalem, besides the punishment of his body, the abnegation of his honor and,

---

4 "Of the conversion of the Magdalene St. Luke writes" [Ex 282]. Explanation of this mystery in F. RAMIREZ, *El Evangelio según S. Ignacio. La Vida de Cristo en los Ejercicios Espirituales y la tradición bíblica en la Vita Christi del Cartujano*, Mensajero-Sal Terrae-U.P. Comillas, Bilbao-Santander-Madrid 2021, 537-559.

5 A. ALBURQUERQUE (ed.), *Diego Laínez. Primer biógrafo de san Ignacio*, Mensajero-Sal Terrae, Bilbao-Santander 2005, 136.

in sum, all humility and asperity. He who wished to please God greatly, it occurred to him to **undertake** these means for his love, for he knew no better ones" [*Life* 9][6].

+ Finally, the work considered definitive about the founder of the Society of Jesus, Pedro de Ribadeneira's *Life of Ignatius of Loyola* (1585), in its Spanish version, does not include the word *conversion* either, although he is the author who in the most detail comments on "disordered" aspects of Ignatius' past:

"He hurried and went ahead, helping himself, in one hand, persevering in his readings [...] and he tried, being very honestly to himself, to change his life and to reorient the 'bow of his thoughts towards a more certain and safer port' than that he had reached till that moment." [*Life*, I, 2 [8]][7].

These first four important testimonies of authors so close to Ignatius of Loyola seem to show a certain detachment from conversion when describing his experience. Verbs such as "he was determined", "he firmly proposed to himself", "he dealt very truly" suggest that the change that took place in Ignatius proceeded more from an act of his free will than from a spontaneous irruption of grace, as would be expected when speaking of conversion.

1.2. Biblical icons of conversion

Mary Magdalene or Paul of Tarsus are the characters to whom the late medieval spiritual tradition looked in order to understand what a case of conversion was: grace received from above, features of otherness,

---

6   J. A. DE POLANCO, *Vida de Ignacio de Loyola* (E. Alonso Romo, ed.), Mensajero-Sal Terrae-U.P. Comillas, Bilbao-Santander-Madrid 2021, 56-57.

7   P. DE RIBADENEIRA, *Vida de Ignacio de Loyola, Fontes Narrativi IV*, IHSI, Roma 1965, 91. Modern English version: *The Life of Ignatius of Loyola* (C. Pavur, trans.) Institute of Jesuit Sources, St. Louis 2014.

divine initiative, certain spontaneity, sudden change of life....

This was not how it happened with Ignatius. His process was slower, meditated, consciously assimilated where the evident protagonism of the "I" was confirming the silent work of grace. The way in which the inner process of transformation took place in Ignatius was different from the way conversion was understood in the spiritual literature of his time. The latter emphasized a sudden and intense irruption of God in the life of the person, who was reoriented in his freedom without being able, on the other hand, to resist or refuse the proposal of the Spirit. Let us look at two icons from the New Testament.

a. The conversion of Paul of Tarsus

The idea and the experience of conversion in the mentality of Ignatius, of his first companions and probably in the spiritual theological environment of his time was closer to what can happen in a first time election as described in [Ex 175], than to what happened to Ignatius, more or less, in [Au 8-14].

Indeed, [Ex 175] describes the first time of election; it exposes in a very brief way how a person can reorient his life in a certain, consistent and indubitable way from a situation "of sin" or contrary to the values of the Kingdom to become a disciple and apostle committed to his Lord from the first line of the following of Christ. Ignatius illuminates this paragraph [Ex 175] with the vocations of Paul and Matthew. But this was NOT what happened in Loyola.

If by *conversion* we understand what happened to Saul of Tarsus on the road to Damascus, it is clear that we cannot understand as *conversion* what happened to Ignatius, because Ignatius and Paul went through different situations, both in their causes (why), in their contents (what) and in their modes (how). The first mode of choice [Ex 175] makes conversion, vocation and choice coincide in the same instant of mystical lucidity due to an irruption or entry of God into the person, which reaches the depths of his being to connect will/affection [experience] with understanding/reason [interpretation of experience] and freedom in act [historicized decision] and all this with an unappealable lucidity, conviction and certainty.

b. The conversion of Mary of Magdala

Another biblical icon of primary importance for understanding what in Ignatius' time was understood by *conversion* is Mary Magdalene. St. Teresa of Jesus explains in these terms: "I was very devoted to the glorious Magdalene, and many times I thought of her conversion, especially when she received communion" (St. Teresa, *Life*, ch. 9). The *Tesoro de Covarrubias* includes this biblical woman to illustrate the meaning of conversion: "Conversion of the sinner, like the conversion of the Madalena"[8]. Ignatius, as we saw, also directly links the Magdalene with a conversion experience [Ex 282], most probably taken from *Vita Christi* I [60]: "On the conversion and penance of the Magdalene". But, again, what happened to Ignatius was not an encounter with the Lord as this Gospel passage reflects.

1.3. "Rereading" the process of Ignatius of Loyola

So, if the first testimonies do not speak of a conversion, what happened to Ignatius of Loyola? By avoiding using the word *conversion* to describe the internal process of Ignatius in Loyola (1521-22), the authors of the time (Laínez, Cámara, Polanco, Ribadeneira) are telling us that what happened there was not a "conversion" in the usual religious

---

8   S. DE COVARRUBIAS, cit., s.v. Convert.

sense of the term, but rather an interior transformation of a person towards a more radical following of the Lord, which evolved amid doubts, shadows, lights, successes and errors; an authentic and Christian transformation, undoubtedly, but one that did not follow the usual or stereotypical paths of conversion, according to the patterns of the 16th century.

Therefore, how does the conversion represented in Mary Magdalene and Paul of Tarsus differ from what happened in Ignatius of Loyola? In three points:

a. The vital and moral state from which the person comes. Ignatius is not situated in the moral sphere of sin as a persecutor of Christians (Paul) or a sinful woman (Mary).

b. In how the relationship with grace and the transformation of the subject takes place. By divine initiative, direct and immediate in Mary and Paul and in close collaboration with the freedom and determination of the subject in Ignatius.

c. How time intervenes in the experience of conversion or transformation: in an immediate way in Mary Magdalene and Paul and in a slower way in Ignatius (9 months).

Then, what should we call what happened in Loyola? It was not a conversion from one state "A" to another "B", but a gradual reorientation in the life of a person who was polarized or attracted in his affection, desire and project by a new horizon that little by little was emerging in his life and that had Jesus of Nazareth as the first and powerful attracting center of energy[9].

---

9 Fr. García Mateo spoke of *mutation*: "The great mutation of Íñigo de Loyola in the light of the Carthusian Vita Christi." *Manresa*, 61 (1989), 31-44.

The action of the Spirit through consolation and the involvement of Ignatius' freedom through his resolutions and determinations were weaving a decision that had no turning back.

Whatever we call it, we must recognize that what happened in Loyola was a "princeps, first, primordial" experience that, on the one hand, assumed the previous trajectory, especially what Ignatius lived in 1517, at the age of 26, and, on the other hand, offered a framework for understanding what Ignatius was going to live in the thirty-five years that remained of his life.[10]

But where did this experience come from, what did it consist of? And where did it point to for his immediate future? Because not everything had begun in Loyola.

2 The Transformation of Ignatius of Loyola

2.1. Phase 1. Depth and density of life. (Arevalo / Nájera 1517)

If the battle of Pamplona occurred in 1521 and Ignatius was born, as we think, in 1491, we can conclude that at the time he was seriously wounded in Pamplona he was 30 years old.

Then the experience of understanding the vanities of the world, the exercise of arms and the vain desire to win honor to which the first lines

---

10 The translator into Basque of the phrase shown in the chapel of conversion got it right: he was not satisfied with choosing the case "norengan" or "norengana" (in this case: Jainkoarengan or Jaikoarengana) but made of it a verb: it is the verb to "orient oneself" vitally not towards a place or towards an idea, but towards the person of God (Jainkoarenganganatu zen). With this verb, the sense of going in this direction here overlaps with the sense of "remaining," of being, we would say, polarized. There is, therefore, a notable difference between "to give oneself up" and "to remain oriented/polarized". Especially if we do not think of the pilgrim and his movement and the fact that God in the first case becomes the receiver (of an offering), and in the second the "magnet" that draws all things to himself.

of the *Autobiography* refer, seems to refer to an experience four years earlier, in 1517. What happened in Íñigo's life in 1517, when then, yes, he was 26 years old? Juan Velázquez de Cuéllar, Chief Accountant of the Kingdom, benefactor and protector of Ignatius, was expelled from the palace of Arevalo and with him all his servants and followers, all his "team", as we would say today, had to leave the Castilian town.

The expulsion from Arevalo marked Ignacio forever. The first "cannonball" that had hit hard on his solid personality did not come from a French soldier, but from a Castilian failure that came to rethink his life. On his way to Nájera, Íñigo experienced a new understanding of a philosophical and metaphysical nature that, most probably, led him to ask himself about the profound meaning of life, about the inexorable passing of time, about the fleeting nature of the present and the density of each instant.

Leaving behind him a courtly, superficial environment, an environment of vanities and appearances, he felt called to reorient his life to begin to live it as an adult and responsibly. Perhaps he realized that life was not a game, but that it is something that "is serious "[11], like the train that only passes once, only one, unique and unrepeatable time. Leaving Arevalo, he would realize that sooner or later we must enter into the Mystery of life, if we really want to understand what this simple and radical sentence "I am alive" could mean.

---

11 Ignatius' first understanding could perhaps be poetically formulated by ceding the word to Jaime Gil de Biedma: "that life was serious / one begins to understand it later / like so many young people I came / to take life ahead of me".

2.2. Phase 2. Life and Mystery of Jesus of Nazareth (May 1521)

This first understanding laid the foundation and enabled Ignatius to receive with generosity and openness this *second understanding* that was waiting for him in Loyola four years later. If his first apprenticeship in La Rioja (1517) helped him to enter into the depths of life, this second one led him to the Source of life itself.

If we analyze the testimonies of his first companions (Laínez 1547, Polanco 1548, Câmara 1553, Ribadeneira 1585) we see that Íñigo experienced a double movement of the heart with respect to the world in which he lived, consolation and desolation[12]. One of the two movements, *consolation*, took the initiative, and soon became responsible for the process. Once initiated, the two walked hand in hand; the two movements alternated one after the other, and oriented the affections in the opposite direction.

Something as simple, as elementary and even as "poor" as the magical exercise of reading, that which today we consider as the most basic level of any education (knowing how to read), became the detonator of a whole psychic and spiritual process that Íñigo could not even imagine and did not even know how to control. In his house in Loyola, says the *Autobiography*, "none of the books he used to read were found, and so he was given a Vita Christi and a book of the lives of saints in romance" [Au 5].

We cannot fail to appreciate the importance of the first reading in the conversion of Ignatius. We can never be sufficiently grateful to Magdalena de Araoz, his sister-in-law, for having offered him some pious

---

12 I have tried to go into detail on the transformation that Ignatius may have undergone from the scarce data we have in J. GARCÍA DE CASTRO VALDÉS, "El proceso de simplificación de Ignacio", *El Dios emergente*, Mensajero-Sal Terrae, Bilbao-Santander 2001, 220-240.

readings "to pass the time" of his convalescence.

The precious text of that Carthusian monk, Ludolpho of Saxonia, who told the stories and anecdotes of Jesus and his disciples, played its role. His words and images gradually captivated Ignatius. Ignatius read and read (1) "by which, reading many times..." he became fond (2) of what he found written until he came to affirm: "*tasting* much of those books"(3) [Au 11].

We can imagine Ignatius, turning the pages of the *Life of Christ*, from one chapter to another, without worrying too much about following a logical order. Once he closed the books, tired of reading, the stories of Jesus came to life in his imagination and fantasy (4), then in his dreams and desires. Íñigo found himself involved in "thoughts" about Galilee, apostles, beatitudes, loaves and fishes, lepers, blind men and Pharisees....

Through his imagination, Ignatius began to experience that a new world, so fascinating and unknown, began to emerge within him, and that it flowed freely through the channels of his psyche and his emotions; but, above all, the most radically new and surprising thing was the *emotional repercussions* (5) that all this began to awaken within him.

The stories of Jesus filled him with life, enkindled his illusion and gave him a new joy that perhaps he had never felt before. To imagine Jesus and with Jesus was already in itself a cause of life and new life. It was different from what court life had been offering him for the last 15 years and what he would later call "delight" or "delectation"[Au 1. 8; Ex 35]. This joy was different.

When fifteen years later in Venice, already in 1536, he will be putting the finishing touches to his precious book the *Spiritual Exercises*, he will write in paragraph 329:

"It is proper to God our Lord and his angels in their motions to give *true joy* and spiritual joy", this is the first rule of discernment of the second week. Ignatius was not speaking from a theory learned in some sermon of St. Bernard, in a lecture of John Cassian or in one of the treatises of John Gerson who influenced him so much. No. Ignatius was speaking from his *experience*, from feelings and motions that can only come from God. God, in giving them, arouses joy, communicates the joy of his presence. It was the first time he had experienced something like this.

Where can we situate this conversion? If the first experience of 1517, leaving Arevalo behind him, was a conversion of philosophical, existential or metaphysical content, this one of Loyola was descending slowly but unstoppably towards the *religious* dimension of his life. What is the difference? The difference lies in the appearance of otherness and transcendence as the horizon of meaning and the Principle and foundation of a whole life. God is here.

If in philosophical conversion the subject finds himself alone before the truth of himself and of his own life, which makes him ask himself "What do I do or what must I do to become a better person?"; religious conversion invites us to ask ourselves: "What do you want from me, Lord, to be a better follower of yours, to remain closer to you?".

Although Ignatius had received a traditional Christian religious formation as a child, religion now began to mean something else. This experience consisted in having personally, experientially and *consolingly* discovered Jesus of Nazareth, Jesus in his humanity, Jesus as Lord, as friend, as companion... Ignatius began to enter into the vital and experiential dimension of religion; he began to "feel and taste" the joy of being with Jesus.

But Loyola's experience was not satisfied with having triggered an affective attraction and fascination for Jesus. Ignatius did not remain paralyzed in his admiration for his new Lord and his Project, but he entered with impetus and energy into the dynamics of imitation and following of Christ without any other support or methodologies than imitating the apostles or the saints of his readings.

Ignatius decided to involve his freedom in a disproportionate and still indiscreet way, "this soul that was still blind" [Au 14]: "he *firmly* proposed to himself to change his life and to give everything to God (although he did not manifest it to any person); he thought and *determined* to *really* do it"[13] [*Life* P. 9] and, in the opinion of friends and relatives, in an indiscreet and imprudent way [cf. Au 12].

Íñigo could have stayed in Loyola and Azpeitia, collaborating actively in the pastoral plan of his parish[14]; he could have dedicated himself to animating the spiritual life of the simple people of the surroundings or to organizing small structures of support and solidarity, charitable works for the most needy, perhaps some kind of NGO of the 16th century.

But no. Íñigo interpreted that in this chapter of his life he had to do something great for Christ and he set his sights on the greatest possible feat: not Montserrat, not even Santiago de Compostela or Rome... he sought to go to the first sources, there where everything had begun: "Jerusalem".

So, what did Ignatius convert to? The question is not the right one. At this point in his life it is more appropriate to ask: *To whom* did Ignatius convert? Above all, it was a conversion to a Person, to Jesus, for whom he felt attraction, fascination and unstoppable friendship. But it was the first and primordial, sufficient and necessary experience that

---

13   The words of Polanco recall those of the Ex 98: "I want and desire and it is my deliberate determination...".
14   Parish of San Sebastian de Soreasu, which his parents ran and financed.

made possible and gave consistency, memory and meaning to the whole subsequent process.

This incipient friendship with Jesus led him to take a gentle distance from what until then had been shaping his world. Allowing himself to be attracted by Jesus led him to distance himself from his past life. Without knowing it, he was entering into what the anonymous author of the 14th century English classic, *The Cloud of Unknowing*, has called the cloud of forgetfulness: "he was already *forgetting* his past thoughts with these holy desires that he had" [Au 10].

The Holy Spirit had done much of the work, perhaps the most difficult work: to disaffect him from the banner of vainglory in order to draw him affectively into the new ecosystem of humility that flowed from closeness to Jesus.

2.3. Phase 3. Reconfiguring the "I" (Manresa 1521-Jerusalem 1523)

We encounter Ignatius converted to the seriousness of life (1517), converted to friendship with Jesus and determined to go to Jerusalem.

But we would be naive, indiscreet and optimistic if we were to say that Loyola's experience had achieved everything. Ignatius lost sight of Itzarraitz (Loyola's mountain) with his gaze fixed on Tabor. But his transformation was not as radical or as total as he himself thought. What he *thought* he had become and what he had *truly become* coincided in part, but it was far from affecting the whole.

The process of configuration to Christ was a longer and more painful task than he could have imagined. Dreaming of Jerusalem, changing his clothes or shoes, buying a pilgrim's staff, growing his nails or hair, or even reorienting his affective-sexual world was not enough to transform a consolidated person into an inner world of worldly values, desires and aspirations. His "I", already 30 years old and with a complex psychoemotional structure, was something harder to conquer than the fortress of Pamplona.

The eleven months spent in Manresa (March 1522-February 1523) confronted him with a whole world of disorders and temptations that the Benedictine monk of Monserrat (Juan Chanones) knew how to accompany with patience, wisdom and prudence.

It is striking to see how, in a few weeks, Ignatius went from an optimism and vital euphoria capable of overcoming every obstacle before one of the most "heroic" undertakings of a pilgrim (Jerusalem), to a radical poverty and misery, submerged in meaninglessness, tempted to suicide and humiliated to the point of being willing to follow a little stray dog, if that could bring him a little light. "Show me, O Lord, where I can find it [relief], for even if I have to follow a little dog to give me the remedy, I will do it." [Au 23].

a. The memory of Jesus, the rock of permanence

Today we are also struck by the fact that this man in love with Jesus, but immersed in such a deep crisis, did not decide to return to Azpeitia. In the middle of the night, the memory of the past would shine brightly. *Why not return home?* The memory of a peaceful and Christian home where he could also live his relationship with Jesus would emerge strongly. *Why not go back?*

The temptation is clothed in good sense and good thoughts: "Íñigo, go back to Loyola, manage properties, attend to the family business; Íñigo, go back to Azpeitia, improve the situation of your fellow countrymen, work for the needy. Your good training in Arevalo can be very effective in Loyola. Íñigo, come back, you can get married, surely some responsible and attractive woman from Azpeitia, Bilbao or San Sebastián could become a good wife; ...". Many thoughts, all good, very human and religiously healthy.

But Íñigo did not return, and this *non-return* also speaks to us of the depth of his experience in Loyola. Why did Ignatius not abandon his project?

Perhaps because he relied again and again on the *consolation* he had felt in Loyola; that *true joy* that could only come from God [Ex 329]. The experience of Loyola inhabited his memory and Ignatius returned to it again and again to discover in the past the light for the present and the meaning of the future[15]. The experience of Jesus that Ignatius had in Loyola was the rock of the foundation of his new life; the waters and the storm came but the house resisted. Ignatius stood the test of the night of meaning and the temptation of abandonment. It was true, it was Truth.

Ignatius did not return because he trusted in what he had experienced; he trusted in his own strength in which he recognized the presence of God. He trusted in the faith that God was still there, even if he did not feel it as the consolation he had sensed in Loyola. The ego and the bad spirit made it difficult, very difficult, but Íñigo's psychology withstood the onslaught.

b. The ego, the hardest and most persistent combat

Meister Eckhart says: "there was never greater virility, greater war, nor greater combat, than to forget oneself and lose oneself."[16] This was the battle that Ignatius now had to fight and that sooner or later is presented to every follower of the Lord. Perhaps the hardest, the conversion

---

15 Resonates the tenth rule of the first week [Ex 323]. The memory of consolation offers energy to go through the trial of desolation: "taking new strength for then".
16 M. ECKHART, *El fruto de la nada*, Siruela, Madrid, 2001, 150.

of one's own love, of one's own judgment... the conversion that demands to surrender one's life and, above all, to surrender oneself. It was easier to reach Jerusalem than to reach the depths of oneself.

b.1 Discerning poverty

Following the example of the saints, Íñigo trusted again and immersed himself in the praxis of an actual, material poverty; a visible, quantifiable, objective poverty. Food, drink, fasting, clothing, sleep and vigils, disciplines and penances... but what in itself can be interpreted as an objective virtue, could also act as a camouflaged impediment to attain the intended holiness.

One could see a man dressed in sackcloth, but what was underneath the rough, coarse cloth? Poor, torn sandals were visible, but what was supporting, or perhaps concealing, this obvious barefootness?

In time, Ignatius realized that such visible and evident poverty also needed to be discerned. This first poverty also contained an "egoic" or self-centered component that could be feeding him a narcissistic ego satisfied by experiencing austerities and sacrifices as so many saints had done.

If he was not careful, I quote the text, "this soul that was still blind... not looking at anything interior, nor knowing what humility was, nor charity, nor patience, nor discretion to regulate nor measure these virtues..." [Au 14], if he was not careful, his own relationship with poverty could be interpreted as one more conquest in his curriculum vitae of victories, nothing further from what he indeed intended, to walk humbly with Jesus and towards Jesus.

b.2 His desire, his way, his purpose... God's way?

In referring to Ignatius, the *Autobiography* speaks frequently of *his* way [Au 17], *his* custom, *his* resolutions [Au 17], *his* firm purpose [Au 45], *his* beads, *his* desired dress [Au 18]. Already in Jerusalem the text insists: "*his* firm purpose [Au 17], *his* intention [Au 45], *his* good intention [Au 46], *his* purpose, that which he would not give up for any fear" [Au 45-46].

The inclusion in the text of this repeated "his" is a deliberate and conscious choice of the author to help us realize that Ignatius is still largely being led by *his* own will and desire, always in process, on the way, in the ever-pending task of overcoming himself and entering (the gerund is important) into the consoled surrender to the Will of God.

Seeking in everything to respond to what God was asking of him, Ignatius learned by observing himself meticulously to distinguish what he would later write in that famous paragraph [Ex 32] of the *Exercises*: "I presuppose three thoughts in me: one that comes from myself, from my mere freedom and will, and two others that come from outside, one from the good spirit and the other from the evil one".

From the analysis of experience, Ignatius learned to separate that which came from his own desire, will and will from that which came from the desire or will of God.

It is the learning that points towards dispossession, towards surrender and, more dramatically, towards our own death. It is the learning to take up the cross every day that guarantees that we do not carry only our desires, our intentions or projects, however evangelical or good they may be or may seem to us, but that we live surrendered to assume with faith the desire, the will, the project and the action of God in us. Our life is not as much ours as we think, it is first and foremost, *His* Life, *His* life in us.

This conversion of the "I", of the "self" has no end, it is an experience of asymptotic character. As our Lord did with Peter, we are open to

Jesus at any moment calling us aside and asking us repeatedly about love: "Íñigo, do you love me?" (Jn 21). Much more important than my own devoted deeds for Christ is to de-center myself from the ego and remain willingly and resolutely in his love, deeds or no deeds, this is secondary.

2.4. Phase 4. The desire and will of the Church (Jerusalem, 1523) [Au 45-48].

This third conversion to the more *anthropological-theological and essential dimension of poverty* acquired a sudden and unexpected new light at the end of September 1523. The Provincial of the Franciscans, custodians of the holy places, threatened Ignatius with excommunication if he did not leave Jerusalem within the agreed time limit and return to his place of departure. Much more than a historical anecdote, no doubt unpleasant for both parties, it was a new shock, as if another new "cannon shot" hit Ignatius and once again invalidated the direction of his new life.

Ignatius had invested two hard years in arriving in Jerusalem with his firm intention [Au 45.46] to remain there; now, after only twenty days of cultural and spiritual visit he had to return to his homeland without the possibility of discussion or dialogue.

It is interesting to note that it is precisely after this new crisis in Jerusalem that the expression "God's will" appears for the first time! in the *Autobiography*; I quote: "after the said pilgrim understood that it was God's will that he should not be in Jerusalem" [Au 50].

With the ecclesial authority, a new variable in the process of Ignatius' conversion burst in with evidence and energy. Until now, the religious experience had two protagonists: Ignatius and Jesus, and these were found in the interiority/subjectivity of the pilgrim, in a close, intimate and affective relationship.

But now Ignatius has to open his experience to a third element, a source of authority not only juridical, but also theological and mystical. But Ignatius does not understand this. In 1523 it was enough for him to obey in order to get out of the way and integrate into his historical moment what the Franciscan provincial indicated to him. In the midst of his bewilderment and his new failure, he accepted the link *Church - obedience - will of God*, but it would still take him some time to understand internally the mysticism that inspired and founded this trilogy.

What he believed until now to be the only and sufficient criterion: the movements (motions) discerned from his interiority, in order to succeed in his particular following of Christ, came to be resized by a higher instance that asked for an urgent step in his discernment processes.

The solid Egoic character of his way of proceeding continued to open up to new ways of understanding the relationship with God, in this case to what he would later formulate as "our holy mother hierarchical Church" [Ex 353].

This Jerusalem crisis opens the way to our next point. The Spirit dosed the elements of conversion according to *Ecclesiastes*: "there is a time for everything and a season for everything under the sun" (Eccl 3:1).

2.5. Phase 5. The Gaze of the Other, the Face of God (Barcelona 1523-Paris 1534)

It seems that Ignatius entered Jerusalem on September 4, 1523 and left the Holy City for Jaffa, to return to Venice, on the 23rd. Barely twenty days had ben enough to dispel the dream in which he had invested so much hope and energy. What happened in Jerusalem and what might this brief lapse of time have to do with the exploration we are doing on the conversion of Ignatius?

We do not have much information about Ignatius' time in Jerusalem. The *Autobiography* surprises us again and devotes only four paragraphs to this episode of Ignatius through the holy places [Au 45-48] and of these, it turns out that the last three (!) are devoted to explaining the conflicts with his departure. Ignatius is very sparing in speaking of his inner experience: "the same devotion he always felt in the visitations of the holy places" [Au 45][17].

To enter into this fifth understanding/conversion we must go back again to Loyola and approach another of "his" resolutions, another of those initiatives that Ignatius took on from the beginning without stopping to think too much about whether or not it was God's will.

On leaving his father's house, Íñigo was convinced that God was calling him to a solitary undertaking, to reorient and restart his life in solitude and to live his newfound vocation in an exclusive relationship with his new Lord, with Jesus.

The *Autobiography* allows us to conclude what we are saying: as soon as he could, "he left his brother in Oñate" [Au 12] and a little later "dismissing [in Navarrete] the two servants who were going with him" [Au 13] he continued on his way to Montserrat; "he set out *alone* on his mule", and later, when already from Barcelona he is on his way to Venice, "although some companies were offered to him, he did not want to go but *alone*" [Au 35] and Ignatius himself seems to explain why:

"because he wished to have three virtues: charity and faith and hope; and taking a companion with him, when he was hungry he would

---

17 Something else we know from Polanco: "he was filled with so much pleasure and feeling of spiritual consolation, that what he had first thought of, he then with much more certainty determined, namely, to remain there" (*Vita*, 82 [30], the only paragraph he dedicates to Ignatius' stay in the Holy Land).

expect help from him; and when he fell, he would help him up; and so he would also trust him and be fond of him in these respects; and that this trust and fondness and hope he wished to have in God alone [...] he had a desire to embark, not only alone, but without any provision" [Au 35].

Now, how long does this desire, *his* desire, to build *his* vocation in solitude last in Ignatius? In my opinion, Ignatius most likely rethought this aspect of his life during his return journey from Jerusalem. Knowing Ignatius, it is very likely that from October 3 leaving Jaffa until mid-January 1524 arriving in Venice (a little more than three months), our pilgrim were remembering and praying, "feeling and tasting internally" all that he had seen and experienced in the Holy Land.

And in remembering... Ignatius understood that going in the same places as Jesus carried the implication of walking in the same places as his disciples. Ignatius understood that Jesus rarely walked alone and that, therefore, to be counted among Jesus' friends and disciples meant to begin to be part of a community, a group.

To think of Jesus and to desire to be part of his friends necessarily meant being recognized as a member of a group, a group of friends, of his disciples, of companions. Although he could not and should not renounce the personal and original relationship that he was building with his Master, he began to understand the social dimension of the following, its collegial, societal structure, its *ecclesial* character.

Yes, it was probably from his experience in the Holy Land that Ignatius rethought and understood his new way and style of being with Jesus. Perhaps he felt resituated, less in a self-centered way of discipleship, but more as a part of a group of followers, of a small church that he would end up calling "Societas Iesu", "Minimal Society of Jesus".

That is why, although so brief, the Jerusalem experience was key in this regard and marks a before and after in Ignatius' way of understanding and understanding himself in discipleship. He had to find companions. Back in Barcelona (1524) and thanks to the generosity of his good friend Isabel Roser, he was able to acquire the level of Latin necessary to be admitted to the University of Alcalá and to begin studies "to help souls", but the time in the city of the Cathedral of the Sea [Barcelona], was also the beginning of the first attempts to consolidate a group of companions.

Barcelona, Alcalá and Salamanca offer not little information about the adventures that Íñigo lived with Calisto de Sá, Diego de Cáceres, Juan de Arteaga and Juan Reynalde, who was called Joanico. Together they lived episodes typical of university students, the first adaptations of the spiritual exercises and other chapters a little harder with the authorities of the Inquisition. We know that they were good friends and loved each other. Ignatius shared a cell in Salamanca with Caceres in a truly uncomfortable situation and all together they planned a new stage of their lives in Paris, but the dream was never realized. "Determined to go to Paris, he agreed with them that they would wait there [Castile] and that he would go to see if he could find a way for them to study" [Au 71].

It is common knowledge that this first group of companions did not succeed; although Ignatius wrote to them frequently [Au 80] from the city on the Seine, none of them went to Paris. "Calixto went to the court of Portugal and from there to the Indies" from where he returned rich; Cáceres returned to Segovia, which was his homeland" and Arteaga died "in a strange accident" having been named bishop in Mexico.

But Ignatius' conversion to the group was another point of no return. He wanted to continue his following of Christ with other companions and so, after a short time of searching in Paris he came to coincide in the college of Santa Barbara with a Savoyard and a Navarrese, Pedro Fabro and Francisco de Jasso, from Javier, who as is well known formed the first nucleus of what twelve years after Ignatius' entry into the Sorbonne would be the Society of Jesus.

After Faber and Xavier, four other companions would join the group. Diego Laínez, Alfonso Salmerón, Nicolás de Bobadilla and Simón Rodrigues. This is neither the time nor the place to dwell on the life of this group, nor to analyze the internal keys to its functioning, nor to compare it with the first group of Alcala. It is enough for us now to affirm that Ignatius' conversion process was joined by this new piece that slowly and silently, but harmoniously, together with all the others, was configuring a new charism in the Church.

This group came to seal their commitment to remain together after their studies in the liturgy of the chapel of St. Denis in Montmartre, outside Paris, and promised to travel together to Jerusalem if circumstances permitted. On that August 15, 1534, none of them could have imagined that 6 years later they would kneel in front of Pope Paul III asking him to recognize them as a new *group* in the Church, a new religious order (one more!) and that they would be sent as missionaries of the pope to unsuspected places.

Perhaps on leaving Paris in early April 1535, on the way to his native Azpeitia, yet another farewell, Ignatius was able to recall the fruitfulness of what he had experienced twelve years earlier as a painful failure in Jerusalem. On the mule that his companions had rented him, he could remember his forced departure from the Holy Land against his will, as the work of a hidden providence that was guiding an itinerary that no longer belonged to him.

From a geographical and temporal distance, that Franciscan provincial, Fr. Marcos de Salodio, appeared to Ignatius as part of a design of

God that never ceased to surprise him.

The failure and death of *his* firm intention to remain in Jerusalem was resurrected in a fruitful period of studies in Paris and, above all, in a group of "friends in the Lord" who had entered his life and his history to remain for ever.

2.6. Phase 6. *"The conversion to the world and its things".*

I have left for the end of this process the conversion called "to the world and its things" because it seems to me that both in the spiritual and mystical process of Ignatius and in his systematic proposal in the *Spiritual Exercises* it constitutes the port of destination towards which he wishes to direct every person who recognizes him-/herself as a disciple of the Lord from this Ignatian perspective.

As in previous conversions in which Ignatius was reorienting his life towards the density of living, towards friendship with Jesus, towards poverty of the heart or towards the other as mediation of the Other, he also experienced a profound turn without return towards the world and its things. What did this conversion consist of?

The starting point. Perhaps inspired by the example of some of the saints, Ignatius felt at the beginning an inclination to leave the world, to make a vital retreat... something in him seemed to suggest insistently that he might leave the world, "take it out of the world"; he wanted to be part of that spiritual current *"fuga mundi"* that encouraged him to find the true meaning of life, peace and with it God, in the silence of some religious cloister or some cave far from any hint of secular bustle.

Let us return to our text. In the *Autobiography*, we read: "And when he had counted what he would do after coming from Jerusalem, he offered to go to the Carthusian monastery in Seville, without saying who he was, so that they would have him as little as possible" [Au 12]. In spite of the fact that Íñigo sent a house servant from Loyola to get information about the rule of the Charterhouse of Miraflores de Burgos, "and the information that he got had seemed good to him" [Au 12], this option, which he still saw as a distant possibility, did not worry him any more.

What did occupy his time and inner space was the search for solitude, to the point of trying to build a personal life project so naively trusting in God that he could dispense with all contact with human structures and means of proceeding: Familiar with palace accounts and budget, Ignatius moved to the other extreme and avoided all possible contact with money; accustomed to living in abundance, he now preferred to live in today without providing for tomorrow; accustomed to having his plots of fame and recognition (his followers on Instagram or Twitter, we would say today), he now preferred to let himself be carried away by the sincere desire to go unnoticed as a way of withdrawing from public scenarios too well known to him.

That stage as a devout anchorite in Manresa was necessary for his personal process, but he soon understood that it was only one more station on the road and the Spirit was pulling him towards other horizons of meaning beyond penitence and excessive [and indiscreet] austerities....

How did this transformation take place? How can we understand this transformation from an initial desire to flee from the world to an institution, the Society of Jesus, turned to the world and its things? All began in a devout walk along the banks of a river, perhaps in August 1522.

Little do we know of that experience known as the "illustration of the Cardoner". As a cognitive and intellectual experience, Ignatius had a metaphysical-mystical intuition in which he understood that "all things seemed new to him" [Au 30]. We could ask Ignatius what this "newness" might have consisted of and what he saw that evening in *things* he had not seen before.

At such an early date, a few months after leaving Loyola, Ignatius could not understand what happened to him as he sat facing the river, although it was one of the experiences that most intensively marked his life and that he would remember as primordial and inspiring one thirty years later in Rome.

In my opinion, this experience of the Cardoner laid the historical-mystical foundation for one of the central elements of the Ignatian-Jesuit charism: its constitutive and structual option for the world, its things and its people; the option for history and time and what happens in them, especially to their inhabitants.

As the years went by, Ignatius changed his way of interpreting the world, moving from an initial look of distrust, suspicion or even a certain fear, to include it as an inalienable element of his spiritual experience. Following Jesus includes *trans-porting* the world with oneself, assuming it as a pneumatological parcel of my Christian responsibility. The world and its things and its diversity of persons... are always something new. "All things seemed new to him" [Au 30, Cardoner] and this newness consists in the loving and divine foundation that inhabits everything and sustains everything.

Ignatius gradually elaborated an implicit spiritual theology about this religation of the world with its Creator or this linking of the Divinity with the things of the World. God looks at the world and by looking at it He loves it, and His love inhabits everything and gives it new meaning.

For a deeper understanding of what we are saying, now we can only point out very briefly two keys. The first is offered to us by the second member of the first part of the definition of consolation that Ignatius offers in paragraph 316 of the *Exercises*: "I call consolation..." Ignatius adds: "and consequently, when no created thing on the face of the earth can love in itself but in the Creator of them all".

For Ignatius, experiencing consolation as an immediate experience of God's love entails a *referral* also as necessary as it is immediate towards the world and its things. To have been reached *in this way* by the love of God implies a loving bond with the world and its things, *all* its things (no created thing... the face of the earth), because from the key of consolation they offer themselves to us in their ultimate identity, in what they truly are, creatures like me, inhabited by the same love that sustains and founds me.

The other key that justifies this turn toward the world and its things, as could not be otherwise, is found in the contemplation to attain love that closes the *Spiritual Exercises* [Ex 230-237]. God dwells, works and labors in this world. This is the point of arrival. Since that first conversion to life in 1517, Ignatius has been integrating two fundamental realities: God and the World. Far from presenting themselves as two components of an irreconcilable dialectic, the relationship with Jesus gently led Ignatius to enter into the creaturely dimension of the world in order to involve "all that he has and possesses" [Ex 234] in its progressive dignification of history. Thus, the mission born of friendship with Jesus (Eternal King [Ex 98]) is directed to the World, where God himself is waiting, filling everything with his Spirit.

Conclusion. 5 points to "reflect on and profit from".

+ Ignatius' experience shows us that God and man sometimes have different hermeneutics: what for the human understanding can be read as a radical failure (wound) for God can be the beginning of a new life full of Meaning.

+ Ignatius' conversion fills us with optimism by making us see that the energy of grace is always greater than the resistance we put up to the Spirit.

+ The conversion of Ignatius encourages us to see ourselves in permanent construction, in a process silently built by the Spirit whose logic we sometimes fail to discover, but which is revealed retrospectively, thus discovering the loving and unrepeatable mystagogy of God with each one of us.

+ The conversion of Ignatius invites us to look at ourselves with patience and mercy and helps us to enter into the time and processes of God, whose Clock, so often, advances at a different rhythm from ours.

+ The conversion of Ignatius, in short, encourages us to live from *consolation* as the Word pronounced by Jesus in the depths of our hearts, the only Word that remains as an Echo in the crisis of meaning, as a Light of memory in the night of Faith.

The Conversion of Ignatius of Loyola and its Psycho-Spiritual Perspective

Yosuke Sakai, S.J.

In 2021, the Society of Jesus and friends observed the 500th anniversary of the conversion of their founder, St. Ignatius of Loyola (1491-1556). However, this commemorative year was not just a superficial festivity focusing on his triumphs. The question arose as to whether, via events surrounding the conversion of a human being who lived in 16th century Europe and who became a saint, we can find within our everyday lives in modern Japan universal messages and insights that have evolved until the present, issues that transcend time and culture. On this occasion, via comparisons with philosophy and theology and through borrowing perspectives from psychology, which happens to be a much more novel academic system, I intend to see how the conversion experience of the human Ignatius and his subsequent spiritual journeys turned out into an experience of 'seeing all things anew in Christ.'

When viewed from the backdrop of its creation, the hallmark of the spirituality of Ignatius is seen to be both mysterious and experiential, besides being practical. Moreover, it values emotions, feelings, and movements of the heart. As Ignatius himself affirms in the *Spiritual Exercises*, what matters, "is not so much knowledge that fills and satisfies the soul, but rather the intimate feeling and relishing of things." In Annotation 2,[1] it is stated that the spirituality of St. Ignatius, and especially the process of discernment, is to look within the heart. Hence psychology in that sense may be a compatible term. One might say that it is a spirituality that stresses the process of discerning and tasting things internally. Prior to anything else, the conversion of Ignatius commenced with his wound on the battlefield and its outcome, namely the agonizing internal pain that he endured. This internal pain, though, evoked within his soul a thirst, which was even more profound.

In this Ignatian year, we often encounter people who use the term 'cannonball' moment. However, that is not to say that a single cannonball evoked a spiritual experience. His cannonball experience was no more than a turning point in his life. According to the New Catholic Dictionary, conversion is a "fundamental transformation in the relationship to God, involving the entire human personality. Here, a person freely accepts the invitation of God. It is an act of faith, wherein an individual personally makes a decision." Cardinal Newman, who was canonized a few years ago, has bequeathed us the following words: "*To live is to change, and to be perfect is to have changed often.*"[2] In other words, "living is changing, and completion is the fruit of unceasingly changing. These words convey the process of conversion in forthright terms.

In Europe and the USA in particular, when speaking of Christian conversion, one gets a strong impression that it refers to those who have grown alienated from Christian life, but later owing to some reason or other they repented and awakened once more to the truths of their faith. However, a large number of Japanese are in situations wherein

---

1 Please see IGNATIUS OF LOYOLA, *Spiritual Exercises* [Ex], translation and commentary by HITOSHI KAWANAKA, 2023. This is the source of the passages from the *Spiritual Exercises* that are cited. The following English translations of the writings of Ignatius have quoted from, SAINT IGNATIUS OF LOYOLA, *Personal Writings*, translated with introductions and notes by JOSEPH A. MUNITIZ and PHILIP ENDEAN, London 1996.
2 Please see J. H. NEWMAN, *An Essay on the Development of Christian Doctrine* (1845) section 2.

they cannot get a feel of Christian culture, in their entire life milieu. There is a great distinction between the Western world, where Christianity is rooted in traditional lifestyles and cultures, and the context surrounding Japan.[3] In Japan, many post-adolescents take their own choice regarding entering Christian life. This differs from conversion as understood in a traditional Western sense, and if anything, it appears to bear a greater likeness to what Wakamatsu Eisuke refers to as the "awakening of spirituality."[4] This differs from the Western understanding of awakening to the truth. The resolve to believe, which is the awakening of spirituality, cannot be fully explained in terms of the traditional Christian conversion experience of the West.[5]

In recent years, immigrants hailing from areas beyond Europe have initiated new religions and lifestyles, and concurrently, owing to the inevitable secularization that persists, time-honored Christian values are waning, and the circumstances encompassing Christian life are experiencing modification. In its place, in situations wherein fresh approaches to spiritual experiences are sought for,[6] people in Europe are clamoring for 'New Evangelization' and "New Catechetics." This state of affairs has

---

3   For example, among the representative Christians of the Meiji era in Japan, we have Uchimura Kanzo. His conversion process commenced with his idealization of the Christian faith (civilization), due to his patriotism concerning the development of Japan. However, in order to understand his disappointment with the reality of American (Christian) society, his anguish of selfishness, the change in his view of Japan by encountering a teacher who led a life of deep faith, and the revelation experience of the atonement of Christ, the context of Japan is crucial. It would be hard for Westerners to understand his experience. In particular, to realize why he refers to his Christian faith as a "Christianity grafted on Bushido," an understanding of the cultural context of Japan leading to the Meiji era, is vital. Also, it differs from the concept of conversion as understood in traditional Christian culture. Please see SATO AKIRA, *Faith and the Day of Kanzo Uchimura: How I Became a Christian* (Bulletin of Hosei University 79, pp. 1-12).
4   Please see WAKAMATSU EISUKE, *Uchimura Kanzo, Apostle of Sorrow*, p. 8.
5   How it differs from the notion of the ego in the West, may be clearly seen in Japanese folk tales and other ancient narratives. Please see *The Japanese Psyche: Major motifs in the Fairy Tales of Japan*, by Kawai Hayao.
6   Please see, K. VALENTA, The Church in the West is in decline-and nationalism won't save it, In *America The Jesuit Review* (July 15, 2021).

evolved owing to skepticism regarding the Church, the growth of secularization, and the arrival of non-Christian immigrants. It may be due to the crises evoked within traditional Christian culture and identity, which are on the verge of change.[7] Nevertheless, the issue we are dealing with now is not merely a mutual sharing of a conversion tale regarding a person's awakening from a dying faith, but rather, to focus upon the multi-layered and prolific transformation process itself.

In this setting, I wish to introduce the thought of the Jesuit Fr. Michael Paul Gallagher S.J. (1939-2015),[8] who insisted on the need for New Pre-evangelization. It precedes Evangelization even more than New Evangelization, not just in Europe and the USA which constitute Christian cultural spheres, but in the entire world as well. According to Father Gallagher, "New Pre-evangelization," is "helping people to be ready for the surprises that might be Christ." It would be like the role of John the Baptist, in guiding people towards the new teachings of Christ. He continues saying, "Jesuits have sense of longer, slower, human, spiritual, gradual journey towards the threshold there might be surprised by God." This undoubtedly has its origins in the conversion process of Ignatius of Loyola himself. That is to say, it is a distinctive feature of Ignatian spirituality. It is imbued with a perception of human beings who live by responding to and resisting Grace, a tradition of accompaniment, of proceeding forward with discernment. In the book, the current Superior General of the Society of Jesus, Fr. Arturo Sosa, writes as follows. "The life of a Christian is a pilgrimage. Getting out of oneself, stepping

---

7   For example, to cite a recent case, His Eminence Cardinal Jean Claude Hollerich, current president of the Council of European Bishops, declared that in the post-corona Church, believers who practice the faith "will be smaller in number, because all those who no longer came to Mass, because they came only for cultural reasons, these 'cultural Catholics' of the left and the right, will no longer come." (Cardinal predicts that the Church in Europe will be 'weaker' after the pandemic, ELISE ANN ALLEN, *Crux,* September 4, 2020).

8   Please see, *Jesuits in Ireland* (https://www.jesuit.ie/videos/michael-paul-gallagher-sj/)

forward, being guided, being accompanied, and being open to surprises."[9] A pilgrimage is an encounter with Christ that transcends hopes and expectations. Ignatius also transcended his expectations and encountered Christ. If such is the case, our role would be to walk along with people so that we may encounter Christ, who truly manifests himself in our everyday lives. New initiatives are vital as having additional value. However, what matters more is to search for and feel the existence and call of God in the living environment and reality that surrounds us. This is something that takes precedence to evangelization. I believe both the society of Japan and the Church need to deal with the issue of Pre-evangelization mutually.

Acquiring a new vision through Christ is something that does not begin until we accept our current reality and situation, and this in fact is the commencement of conversion. The call to acquire a new vision through this conversion experience of Ignatius is an impetus towards experiencing encounters and exchanges with Christ, within the reality of our everyday living. Pope Emeritus Benedict XVI once made the following remark. "Conversion is something definitive, decisive, but the fundamental decision must develop, be brought about throughout our life." (January 30, 2008, A talk given before a general audience). Conversion is not a one-time event but a process and path for us to progress onwards. Having this awareness in mind, let us see what possibilities await us within the conversion process of Ignatius.

Originally, psychology by nature was viewed as unrelated to faith, doctrines, or the corroboration of spiritual experiences. Nevertheless however, in the context of individual or group psychological realities,

---

9   Please see, A. SOSA, *In Cammino con Ignazio*, p. 19.

psychology comes in useful regarding the attaining of a more profound grasp, as to what it means to believe. James Fowler (1940-2015), a theologian who explored the connection between human growth and faith asserts, "Faith is an orientation of the total person, giving purpose and goal to one's hopes and strivings, thoughts and actions." Hence, "faith is an integral part of one's character or personality."[10] As stated here, there exists a significant affiliation between human growth, development, and faith. Religious conversion is a process whereby one believes, converts, and practices.[11] In that sense, in order to think of religious conversion, we need to take a frank look at humanity, which is not in a condition of pre-established harmony, and ponder over events of encounter between man and God.

Recently, the field of psycho-spirituality has attracted attention. While dealing with the human heart, psychology deals in parallel with links to transcendental existences and spiritual values. The liaison between faith and psychology is far from being a liaison of confrontation. Rather, it is becoming clear that to gain an understanding of human beings in the presence of God, it is a relationship that cannot be ignored. This, however, is by no means a new idea. The 13th century theologian Thomas Aquinas presented his famous definition, *Gratia non tollit naturam, sed perficit,* (ST, I, I, 8 ad 2), or "Grace does not destroy nature, but perfects it." Also, as the Church Father St. Irenaeus stipulated, "The glory of God is the human person fully alive." In humanity as a created being, the glory and grace of God are made manifest. In the 16th century, long before psychology was known, Ignatius of Loyola, recognizing the movements of his heart and the spirits that work both implicitly and explicitly, systematized a form of prayer to choose a way of life and discov-

---

10 Please see, J. FOWLER, *Stages of Faith*, pp. 14, 92.
11 Please see, R. F. PALOUTZIAN, *Religious Conversion and Spiritual Transformation*, p. 331.

er the will of God. St. Paul once affirmed, "when I am weak, I am strong." Similarly, when human beings concede that they are weak, fragile, and devoid of strength, they become aware of the power granted them by the Transcendent. St. Augustine also declared, "You have made us for yourself, O Lord, and our hearts are restless until they rest in You." (*Confessions*, 1, 1, 59). In today's language, this would say that when one faces doubt or suffocation in life and receives spiritual accompaniment or counseling, it is not merely an issue of confronting oneself. Even if one does not have a complete perception of it, it is as though one is starting to acquire an experience of something within oneself that transcends oneself.

According to religious psychologist William James, conversion is the process by which a self previously divided and consciously wrong inferior and unhappy becomes unified and consciously correct and happy, in consequence of its more solid grasp upon religious realities.[12] For example, in the case of conversion during the period of adulthood, when viewed from the standpoint of psychoanalysis,[13] the personality traits do not appreciably change.[14] More than a change in nature, what occurs after religious conversion is an alteration in the way in which each disposition is expressed. That is to say, the person discovers a new

---

12 Please see, WILLIAM JAMES, *Varieties of Religious Experience*, p. 171.

13 According to EDWIN STARBUCK (1866-1947), the author of *Religious Psychology*, the optimum age for conversion is adolescence, around the age of 16. More than mental awakening, the motive to escape from sin is stronger. This is linked to what other psychologists state, as for example Jung's Midlife Crisis, Erikson's Identity Crisis, and Maslow's Peak Experience. (Please see the New Catholic Encyclopedia). For example, Horie Norichika writes as follows: "In the case of Maslow and Jung, the ego is something else. In the case of Maslow, the target is the other, namely the world and so on, and in the case of Jung, it is an unconscious image having content that guarantees the ego. The experience of facing the ego and causing it to collapse, is a vital opportunity for self-actualization.

14 Please see COSTA &MCCRAE, 1994, *Set Like Plaster? Evidence for the Stability of Adult Personality*. In T. F. HEATHERTON & J. L. WEINBERGER (Eds.), *Can Personality Change?* Washington, DC: American Psychological Association.

meaning in his reasons for living, his standard of values, his attitudes, beliefs, and identity.[15] The self-realization that occurred via the conversion of Ignatius, was indeed a process of transformation that commenced with the experience of frustration he suffered on the battlefield and sickbed, namely the "death of an inflated ego." Subsequently, by way of his encounters and companionship with Christ (a mysterious communication), he formed a fresh purpose in life, and acquired a new standard of values, new attitudes, new beliefs, and a new identity.

The experience of religious conversion generates a spiritual transformation.[16] In the process of spiritual transformation, there arise gaps between desires, beliefs, and reality, and there arise also variances between "should" and "is."[17] Yet, without these variances and gaps spiritual transformation would be impossible. When critical queries related to life are directed against people, those who are in the midst of such experiences at times tend to reject their faith, because they find themselves unable to answer those queries by using words having meanings that they have been familiar with so far. When striving in the midst of undesired results or painful experiences, people at times seek to overcome the situation by finding new meanings to words. At the battle at Pamplona, young Ignatius believed in attaining victory, and he had no doubts about achieving it. Nonetheless, he suffered defeat, and besides, he also suffered the added shame of being struck by an enemy cannonball and retreating from the battlefield. All the same, however, Ignatius perhaps prayed for the full recovery of his injured leg, envisioning himself once more as a standing man in Court and fiercely active on the battlefield.

---

15 Please see R. PALOUTZIAN, *Religious Conversion and Spiritual Transformation*, In *Handbook of Psychology of Religion and Spirituality*, pp. 332–333.

16 Ibid. p. 334

17 P. C. HILL, *Spiritual Transformation: Forming the Habitual Center of Personal Energy*. In *Research in the Social Scientific Study of Religion* (Vol. 4, pp. 159-182 (2002)).

However, since the surgery happened to be unexpectedly problematic, his leg did not return to its original state. Finding himself in a situation where he could not force himself through, he steadily began to accept his situation as "this is what it is" from "this is what it should be." While striving to urge himself forward, he slowly realized the Transcendent, who speaks to the heart. The young Ignatius was compelled to change his meaning of life. He realized that his preconceived notion that "this is how it should be" was the work of the evil spirit, which impedes a flexible frame of mind, who makes a person meekly accept what he is, and who prevents him from being open to an invitation by God to accept something new. On the contrary, admitting that "this is how it is" was an inspiration from the Spirit of God, which provides people with an opportunity to change and grow. This was the commencement of the spiritual conflict that Ignatius of Loyola experienced, and viewed from this angle, we see that the experience of Ignatius did not vary much from modern psychology.

W. W. Meissner, S.J. (1931-2010)[18] is a Jesuit priest and analyst who dealt with religious themes from a psychological standpoint, particularly psychoanalysis. When asked as to what could be done by multiplying the spirituality of Ignatius with psychoanalysis, he replied that it would lead to a better perception of the spiritual viewpoint of Ignatius.

---

18 Oskar Pfister and William James are pioneers in the study of religious psychology, or faith and psychology. Pfister was a direct disciple of Freud and an analyst-Protestant minister. His and Freud's letters are a key resource to comprehend religious psychology, with an analytical approach. According to TILMAN HABERMAS & CYBÉLE DE SILVEIRA, *Development of Global Coherence in Life Narratives across Adolescence*, in *Developmental Psychology*, 44 (3), pp. 707-721 (2008), the major link between the subjective explanation of human growth and the personality of the individual was studied by therapists, as in the case of Freud's study of Hysteria cases (1905). It was studied by personality psychologists (ALLPORT, 1942; MCADAMS & PALS, 2006), as the basis for using autobiographical material as a comprehensive source of personal information. Among them, Erikson's work on Luther and Gandhi is the first detailed study to show that the development of subjective life stories is significantly allied to the attainment of a mature psychological identity. See page 707.

By a deeper enquiry into the thinking of Ignatius, we can gain an understanding of aspects of his spiritual growth and human effort.[19] That is the reason why more than the spiritual or religious aspects of the achievements of saints, Meissner evinced an interest in issues such as the milieu surrounding saints and their rapport with others, the human inspiration in their spiritual progress, their conflicts, their developmental influences, and their aims in life.[20] By this means, an Ignatius who is much more profoundly human, appears before us. What I endeavor to do here is like an extension of those attempts.

The self is the consequence of the narrative of human life. Here, by delving into the story of the life of Ignatius, I shall seek to clarify as far as possible his depth, the values of his lifestyle, and his virtues.[21] The documents penned by Ignatius, or the official documents concerning him, may be broadly classified into six groups.[22] Among them however, the one wherein Ignatius personally refers to his conversion experience, is his "Autobiography." However, as the first material, there are specific

---

19 W. W. MEISSNER, *Transformative Processes in the Spiritual Exercises*, In *Psyche and Spirit Dialectics of Transformation* (W. W. MEISSNER and CHRIS R. SCHLAUCH) University Press of America, 2003, p. 120.

20 MEISSNER, *"Psychoanalytic Hagiography: The Case of Ignatius of Loyola"* (*Theological Studies* 52, 1991, p. 3).

21 Please see, D. MCADAMS, *The Psychology of The Life Stories*, in *Review of General Psychology*, 5 (2), pp. 100-122 (2001). McAdams says that narratives and life studies generally have 6 principles in common. (1) The self is described. (2) The story integrates life meaningfully. (3) The story is narrated within social relationships and understood as a social phenomenon. (4) The story changes in accordance with time. (5) The story is a cultural text. (6) Some stories have excellent content that communicates moral points of view. These attributes are visible even in the story of Ignatius.

22 The documents Ignatius left behind, or the public documents related to him, can be broadly classified into six groups. The first is the Spiritual Exercises. We also have the "Jesuit Constitutions," concerning the regulations and governance of the Society of Jesus, and the "autobiography" that we are now dealing with. Next, we have the many letters of Ignatius that remain with us. These constitute a record of the contact he had as Superior General, with the Jesuits who had been dispatched all over the world, a notification of his decisions and his replies to consultations. Besides, we have what is referred to as the "Spiritual Diary of Ignatius." Herein are recorded various spiritual experiences he had, while residing in Rome as the Superior General. Finally, there is an official document that was left during his canonization.

points we need to bear in mind concerning the autobiography. First, this autobiography was dictated to and transcribed by his disciple, Fr. Luis Gonzalez da Camara, and so it cannot be said to be a work free of all editing by da Camara.[23] In other words, it is an issue of credibility. In his preface to *Ignatius of Loyola's Autobiography and Diary*,[24] Fr. Francisco J. Osuna, an expert on Ignatian spirituality who once resided in Japan, wrote the following thought-provoking statement: "Even though Ignatius had informed da Camara clearly and in detail concerning his frivolous life during the period of his youth, and after having separated it from other periods, yet these first 26 years of his have been reduced to just a few lines. Was that due to his excessive respect for Ignatius? Or was it perhaps because he wished to maintain the plan of the story? In any case, the anecdotes and events of that time that intrigued us were lost forever." (p.10) It is reported that da Camara from a young age had a strong tendency to idealize Ignatius.[25] At any rate regarding getting to know the course of his life, there exists no narrative surpassing the autobiography, for it provides us with the living voice of Ignatius. In it are revealed, Ignatius as an anxious young man who has undergone a conversion experience and his later life, where he refers to himself as a pilgrim. Hereafter I shall call him by his real name, which is Íñigo, the name he had before its alteration. Let us now embark upon the story of

---

23 Please see, L. G. DA CAMARA, *Memorial*, p. 356. (Japanese translation by J. M. VARA, *Notes of disciples who witnessed the days of Ignatius.*)

24 A. EVANGELISTA, translated into Japanese by TAKASHI SASAKI, 1966, Katsura Shobo.

25 With regard to this characteristic of Da Camara, the following has been written. "He was unaware of the potential weaknesses of Ignatius, and even if he noticed them, he interpreted them in the light of his criteria for idealizing him···his attitude, which made the Saint appear far away in the eyes of members living with him, was it the outcome of his innate hard work, or was it just a masquerade? In some cases, Da Camara could not discern this rather ambiguous attitude on the part of Ignatius. (DA CAMARA, translated by J. M. VARA, "*Notes of disciples who witnessed the days of Ignatius,*" p. 12, J. M. GRANERO, "*El Memorial*" *Da Camara, Manresa* 39 (1967), p. 75).

the conversion of young Íñigo, particularly at Loyola and Manresa.

In speaking of the background of Íñigo, we need to present details relating to the area called Basque. Basque people are possessed of a complex psychology with values related to the individual and group, which at first sight may appear conflicting. It is said that in the Basque country many sailors are sent to sea, and the people too are characterized by a strong sense of patriotism. They are a forest people who are rooted to the land, and they are proud of their ability to dwell in the mountains. They are endowed with a unique life culture that comprises the natural settings of both the seas and mountains, and by utilizing these, they have led sturdy lives. The impact of this natural and historical ambiance of the Basque area upon its residents, has been immeasurable.[26] Íñigo in that sense was an inspiring Basque, who was shaped by that unique culture and by those times. These terrestrial and cultural facets had perhaps influenced the fact of his having noticed the contrast between the conflicting forces that arose within his mind, and what's more, tensions between personal and group missions and so on, are common issues that still arise among the Jesuits.

Let us now consider the situation within the Loyola family, when Íñigo was born. He was born in 1491 to the aristocratic Loyola family in Gipuzkoa, as the youngest of 13 brothers and sisters. His father's name was Beltrán, and his mother was Mariana, and shortly after birth he was baptized and given the baptismal name of St. Íñigo of Oña. This clan, which served the Kingdom of Castile, was small, and yet for generations it was a prestigious family. Even though there was no pressure

---

26 The writer Shiba Ryotaro speaks of the Basques as follows. "Even though they are patriots, they are not just nationalists having the reverse of an inferiority complex. Along with the beauty of the Basque hills and waters, I thought this was a nice aspect of the Basque frame of mind. (*Going on the Highway, Namban no Michi I*, (*The Road of the Southern Barbarians I*).

exerted on the youngest child Íñigo to succeed to the family name, nevertheless it is believed that the expectations and values of leading a life that would not bring shame to the Loyola family, were planted there. One would naturally think that this had an unavoidable effect upon the ego of Íñigo.

His mother Mariana died when Íñigo was still young, and so until the age of 7 he was entrusted to the care of a village woman and raised by her. When Íñigo was 7 years of age his brother Martin married, and his sister-in-law Magdalena entered the castle. He thereupon was brought back to the castle, and until he departed as a page at the age of 16, Magdalena was his foster mother. Magdalena later became deeply involved in the life of Íñigo, and particularly in his conversion experience. Early loss of parents is an event that exerts a great impact on children. One wonders how acute the feelings of bereavement and pain were that young Íñigo suffered. Not only was he forced to endure the early loss of a mother, an object of unqualified love and trust, but he was compelled also to live away from home. His intense feelings of longing for his late mother as well as his love for his foster mother, may both perhaps be glimpsed in the complex and volatile image of the adolescent Íñigo, particularly about his involvement with women and the craving he had for them.

In his *Autobiography* it is said, "Until the age of twenty-six he was a man given up to the vanities of the world, and his chief delight used to be in the exercise of arms, with a great and vain desire to gain honour." [Au 1] After the death of his father, around the age of 15 or 16 Íñigo became a page to Juan Velázquez, who oversaw the Court's monetary audit. It is no wonder that a feeling as though he lacked something had arisen within young Íñigo's heart, upon his removal from the green Basque region he was familiar with, and his being consigned to dreary

Castile. It is not hard to imagine either that the pushy and starry life he later led at Court, was his way of offsetting this loss.[27] While acquiring training as a page, he relished life by reveling in duels, gambling, and women, a life of ambition and desire, and he was concurrently smitten with the King's sister, the Infanta Catherina, an individual whose status differed vastly from his own. In 1517, on the death of Velázquez, he shifted to the service of Antonio de Manrique, the Governor-General of Navarre, who was a full-blooded soldier, and for Íñigo it was no longer Court life but life on a battlefield. This was the setting at the time of his arrival in Navarre in 1521, for his battle with the French.

On examining the personality of Íñigo, who appears to have been imbued with a robust ego, we note that he was in possession of two personality-style traits, namely obsessive-compulsive and narcissistic. Traces of these two distinctive styles may be glimpsed in his conduct and attitude, from his youth until his later years. For instance, we may say that at the battle at Pamplona one gets a good sign of his personality, for in his ego paradigm, grandiosity (a sense of superiority) and self-love (narcissism), are both visible.[28] Meissner calls this a narcissistic personality. Its characteristics are high ideals. It is forward-leaning posture revealing a desire to succeed and perform something great, a feeling of omnipotence, invulnerability, a lack of hesitancy with regard to taking risks for the sake of heroic ideals, and a desire to surmount what appears impossible. More than in normal times people possessed of this personality are effective in emergencies, such as in times of war.

Íñigo then headed for the so-called Pamplona uprising, which was the final battle in the Navarre civil war, and on May 20, 1521, while he

---

27 Please see, A. MUNITIZ, *St. Ignatius of Loyola and severe depression*, *The Way* 44/ 3 2005, p. 60.
28 Freud calls this sentiment a castration horror.

was on his own side of the battlefield, he received a wound on his right foot.[29] Consequently, instead of decorating his hometown with brocade, the wounded Íñigo was brought to his castle of Loyola, thanks to the warmth and care of the enemy soldiers. The fact that he had not only failed to win the battle but had also failed to die, must have been a source of endless vexation for him. His right leg which was crushed by the impact, needed immediate surgery. For Íñigo, to whom appearances mattered more than they did for average men, his greatest wish was to get his feet restored at all costs, so that he might serve once again at Court and perform bravely on the battlefield. It was an era when surgery was performed without anesthesia, and in his autobiography, it is stated that all through the surgery he endured the ordeal with firmly clenched fists, and without uttering a word. On the conclusion of the surgery though Íñigo expressed discontent at the sight of his re-united leg, and so, regardless of the intense pain, he asked them to perform the surgery once more. At that point he had not yet come to accept the realities of "should" and "is." Since he was able to endure such pain, he clearly was a person gifted with singular will power, and other aspects of his strong ego ideal were his resolve to advance without faltering in order to fulfill his aims, and his courage in displaying a disdain for setbacks. Yet, at this point, Íñigo's strong mental powers were for purposes

---

29 In Japanese history, an individual who was also possessed of this characteristic was Oda Nobunaga. In the book the "History of Japan" by Luis Frois, the following is written about Nobunaga. "It is undeniable that Nobunaga was an outstanding person, a person rarely seen. As an unusual and distinguished captain (commander) he ruled the world with great wisdom. He was of medium height, slender in body, and did not have much of a beard. He had a fine loud voice, a great fondness for war, he was devoted to military discipline, he was very honorable, and he was strict with regard to justice." This is merely speculation, but if Íñigo had not been wounded, aside from his faith and religion he might have become a person like Nobunaga. At that time, Nobunaga too who was unafraid of gods or buddhas, aimed for absolute power. In fact, one might perhaps say that he had a strong self-love, and his life was a life spent in battling the fear of castration.

of his dreams, for the reclaiming of ambitions that he had envisioned on his own. They were so to speak, impelled by narcissistic desires. The surgery was relatively effective, but yet his right leg was a little shorter than the left, and that was the reason why since that time, he tended to walk by dragging his leg.

After the operation, as he was unable to walk freely, he had nothing to do and time to spare, and so he passed time daydreaming. In order to cheer himself he asked for a tale concerning knights, but no such book existed in the castle of Loyola, which, in the absence of her husband was managed by his devout sister-in-law, Magdalena. Instead, however, something wholly different, namely two devotional books were handed over to him, namely, "The Life of Christ" (*Legenda Aurea / Golden Legend*) by Ludolph of Saxony, and "The Lives of Saints" (*Flos Sanctorum*), which was widely read at that time in the Iberian Peninsula. His encounter with these two books provided a new orientation to the life of Íñigo.

The *Autobiography* states that the Virgin Mother and Child appeared at the sickbed of Íñigo. Could it not be said that what he unconsciously saw in the Virgin Mother and Child, was an idealized form of his kindly sister-in-law Magdalena and himself? Later Ignatius would refer to the Virgin Mother reverently as "Our Lady" (Nuestra Señora). Magdalena, who had raised him on behalf of his own mother, must have been a unique individual, who evoked within him an awareness of the Virgin Mother. During his post-operative period of healing, his rigid and self-loving ego steadily began to soften, when the strain of the image of his intimidating father was substituted by the gentle, generous, and devout Magdalena. In that sense, for Íñigo who could scarcely raise himself up, it was perhaps a return to his infant days, when he enjoyed the utmost confidence.

These two personality styles constitute vital factors, with regard to gaining a grasp of his conversion experience. I wish to repeat here that grace is not something that excludes nature. On the contrary, it fulfills it. As a person progresses through life, even if no change is visible in his temperament or personality, yet he learns how to compromise between the maturity peculiar to himself, and the reality he confronts. Via the workings of grace his process of maturity began to endow Íñigo with a new form of the self, although the fact remained that it was still ambitious. He went on a pilgrimage to Jerusalem despite the fact it was deemed a risky venture at that time. He believed that since St. Dominic and St. Francis had done so, he would be able to do so as well. His citing of these two great saints as exemplars, indicates that his ego ideal was still relatively strong, as otherwise their names would not have issued from his lips. Let us now probe some stimulating features in the alterations that occurred within Íñigo, at that time.

Dreams of stories concerning knights that once thrilled him did not last long, and in due course, he began to suffer isolation and anxiety. On the contrary, however, he began feeling heartened and consoled on recalling the witnesses of the saints. He integrated the testimony of model saints into his ego ideal. Around this time, one may say that a state of turmoil arose within Íñigo when the values he had earlier nurtured at Court and on the battlefield began to merge with the new values he had now attained. Also, he was still ensnared at this phase of his life by outward triumphs, and his narcissistic overlook was still relatively high. The difference in the movements of the heart, which oscillated between the working of two spirits, was a conflict that was sparked off by the differences between his own two sets of values. It appears at first, Íñigo's ego sought to blend the newly introduced spiritual values into his old narcissism and moderately reconcile those two heterogeneous sets of values. However, as his perception of the new value of following Christ began to deepen within him, he appears to have gradually concluded that it was unviable. Strong feelings of self-love and self-dedication evoked conflicting tensions within him. Íñigo thereupon steered away in stages from the earlier ambitious values of his life, those self-loving, youthful ideals, into a purer, higher, and more profound spiritual course.[30] More than imitate the saints, he sought a way of life that was his own.[31] In other words, for Íñigo, a fresh awareness and perception steadily began to overtake his reality and genuine ideals, and in this way arose a spirituality typical of Íñigo, one that was neither Dominic's nor Francis's.

His *Autobiography* declares, "God was dealing with him in the same way as a schoolteacher deals with a child, teaching him." [Au 27] He may have been an elementary school student, yet in reality was he not perhaps more like an infant? As an aid to understanding this, I wish to use the concept of "Good enough Mother" by the British analyst Winnicott. According to him, newborn infants are at the edge of anxiety.[32] A "Good enough Mother" adapts as much as possible to the needs of the infant and provides it with feelings of unity and omnipotence. In time, as the infant's abilities develop, they slowly provide it with a sense of reality.[33] What we mean by reality is the fact that the mother (caregiver), does not meet all the needs of the infant. A mother who can do this, is what Winnicott refers to as a "Good enough Mother,"[34] and the infant

---

30 In the *Spiritual Exercises*, in the "Rules for thinking with the Church," the 12th rule says, "We must avoid making comparisons between those of our own day and the blessed of former times." Are these also words reflecting his younger days?

31 Please see, MEISSNER, *Psychoanalytic Hagiography*, p. 32.

32 Please see, WINNICOT, Translated by SADANOBU USHIJIMA, *Psychoanalytic Theory of Emotional Development*, 1977, p. 59.

33 Please see, WINNICOTT, translated by MASAO HASHIMOTO, *Playing and Reality*, 1979, p. 14.

gradually comes to know that its sense of unity and omnipotence is an illusion. However, without regaining a sense of security, the disillusioned infant will not be able to live. Space is needed between the infant and the mother, in order to create a sense of security that is nurtured by both of them. Within this space the infant's omnipotence is destroyed, and it once again begins to respond to real objects. Thus, from a dim experience that does not pass through a sense of omnipotence, the infant steadily begins to attain a grasp of reality, which does not move the way the infant would like it to. Winnicott refers to this latent space as an "intermediate area," which is located between the internal omnipotence and external reality. The intermediate area displays its real power in acting as a cushion when facing realities that are hard to accept, and in that way, it enables the making of rational decisions, in conformity with reality. At this time, prior to getting in touch with the real world, objects that provide peace of mind are required in the intermediate area, as for example dolls or toys. These are referred to as "transitional objects." The rapport the infant develops with the mother and the transitional object, enables it to realize that its external world (the world at large) is a secure place. In other words, it is a place and time that plays the role of a bridge. This "initial sense of security" that is fostered during infancy, would for instance play the role of what Erik Erikson refers to as "Basic Trust," and this basic trust is believed to be greatly linked to human growth and development.[35]

I have used technical terminology here, and it may be easier to comprehend their significance if we applied them to the case of Íñigo. He, who was seriously injured and whose dreams were shattered, was

34 Ibid. p. 17.
35 Please see, OKUDA HIDEMi, <Belief>, *The Foundations of Attitudes: Clues to Basic Trust, Habitus,* 18: 131-143.

greatly disillusioned. Since he was unable to move, everything had to be done for him by his sister-in-law Magdalena and others. We may say that for Íñigo, the "Good enough Mother" was Magdalena, and throughout his conversion experience, God seems to have been the one to play that role. Íñigo's emotions of reassurance, consolation, and letdown were desolate, and he suffered those experiences regarding his human relations and the workings of the spirits. In order to pass the time, he requested a chivalric romance in the place of a toy, but his sister-in-law Magdalena, who had nursed him like a mother, denied his request. He was given instead a book on spirituality, a subject in which he had not the slightest interest, and this was for him an added cause for disenchantment. His sense of omnipotence and control, combined with his earlier ambitions, acquired a hazy and misty form. For example, within him were beliefs that brimmed over with omnipotence. These included his bloated ideas of Catholic Spain, his over-idealized Princess Catherine, and his dreams of himself in Court or on the battlefield, and they even went so far as to include St. Francis and St. Dominic.

Nevertheless, however, he had not yet been outdone by reality. His dreams and goals collapsed, and his days of recovery at Loyola and Manresa turned out to be the period between his getting injured and becoming a pilgrim. For the young Íñigo, it was perhaps an interim space, wherein he proceeded towards a new reality and became a pilgrim. It was a time for him to rectify his consciousness while heading towards a reality he had never seen.

For Íñigo, the time in bed as a "helpless child" was like a healthful seedbed, a time and place where he could regain his life, discover a reason for living, and foster trust. During this period, the basic trust that was nurtured by the love and support of the family which he experienced once again served as a boost for him, who was on the verge of despair, and opened for him a world replete with fresh possibilities. God also had a timely involvement with the lost Íñigo, at times at close quarters and at times from afar, and this was accompanied by purifying challenges and solace.

In our lives too, we each possess a unique intermediate space. Placing the new reality before our eyes, it is time for us to prepare for it, even if it be done in a chaotic way. In this present age, when we are tossed around by the corona pandemic, it is possible that it might become an intermediate space that is common to all mankind. Yet, what is vital here is the fact that this intermediate space is not a permanent entity, and sooner or later the "transitional object" will replace reality. When the time finally comes, we will have to let go of what is past. On the other hand, however, to be free of attachments (disordered attachments), is referred to in the human sense as growth or development, and in the spiritual sense as spiritual transformation. This intermediate space can be viewed as an essential experience for maturity. This is what is referred to in Number 155 of the *Spiritual Exercises* as making a choice of the "third class of men," in order to better serve God. Íñigo was not always like an elementary school child. As a pilgrim, he came to walk on his own feet. It was something superfluous, but Christ was the Alpha and Omega. We are protected by God. He is the beginning and the end, and we exist in the middle. Our life in this world may also be occurring in a finite intermediate space, with reference to eternal life.

In his classic on religious psychology entitled, "The Varieties of Religious Experience," James specifies that the experience of conversion involves two extreme states of mind. One comprises the consciousness of sin, imperfection, regret, and a lack of self-confidence, while the other is a positive ideal that embraces a desire to be reborn. However, in many cases, the consciousness of sin being strong exerts a negative influence on the person and becomes an obsession. When such negative emotions grow strong, people naturally get seized by feelings of guilt and anxiety, to the extent that their emotions, reason, and body get overcome. Indeed, the backdrop to the series of negative feelings that Íñigo experienced, and which extended to the point of his even contemplating suicide, can to an extent be explained in this way. It was not a question of his seeking to eliminate the mistakes he had made in the past, but rather, to face life by presenting himself as he was. This was the only choice he had. He realized that God came first, and he had no choice but to gain experiential knowledge of the Merciful God, who was out to find him.

While striving to become perfect, Íñigo's nerves entered a negative loop that began to rage, and the backdrop to this may have been the concept of God he had at that time. On observing the figure of Íñigo striving to subdue himself, we see that the image of a harsh God existed in his mind. Regardless of whether it was an image of his father, an image that had evolved as an outcome of the stresses within the Loyola family, or a reflection of the social situation linked to the national land restoration movements of that time, in any case, the image of God young Íñigo possessed was that of a God of Justice. However, it was of a God who was rather punitive, a terrifying God who did not overlook the minor sin. What he experienced at Loyola was not just the fact of his being monitored and shielded by the gentle Virgin and Child or the face of the compassionate God via his sister-in-law Magdalena. The tension and variation between light and darkness in his God concept can also be perceived in his conversion experience. For instance, to compare Ignatius with Martin Luther would make an interesting study. A simple comparison is not possible, but they both lived around the same period, and notwithstanding the cultural differences between Northern Europe and the Iberian Peninsula, both when young had a strong leaning towards perfectionism and suffered from the image of God they possessed. In the case of one, the mystical experience of encountering Christ was sublimated into a system of prayer, while the other was led on to a conviction of doctrine (Sola Fide). This contrast is also interesting.

Specifically, during his period at Manresa, his inborn perfectionist tendency raised its head, and Íñigo became neurotic. The characteristic symptoms of this can also be read in his *Autobiography*.[36] At one time in Manresa, Íñigo appears to have suffered from what we would refer to in modern times as depressive symptoms. In his *Autobiography*, it is said, "finding himself sometimes so much without relish that he found no savour either in praying or in hearing mass or in any other prayer he made." [Au 21] Also, "here he came to have many problems from scruples." [Au 22] Depression is anger directed against oneself. Hence at Manresa Íñigo suffered over the sins he had committed in the past and fell into states of dejection several times. In the light of the modern Diagnostic and Statistical Manual of Mental Illness (DSM-5), we know that the Íñigo of those days suffered at least from moods of depression, loss of concentration, loss of appetite, loss of energy, he faced complications in making decisions, he suffered from a loss of self-esteem, excessive guilt, and finally he even attempted suicide. The anxiety that attended his delusions pertaining to his salvation, and the crises he suffered, included spiritual, psychological, and physiological content. For example, while at Manresa, Íñigo kept his hair uncut and allowed his finger and toenails to grow. What he saw at that time was an illusion that plagued his heart. Being in this world is no more than living and

---

36 Please see, A. GIDDENS, *Modernity and Self-Identity*, 1991, Cambridge. The author develops his theory in grown-up humans. He includes not just children but also neurotic adult patients.

having a body. A life of belittling physical things and imposing excessive abstinence and sacrifice filled his heart with desolation. It was no more than letting go of the tension of living.

Living is concrete and physiological. Eating, having concern for our surroundings, and interacting with others all involve some internal and external tension.

"Here and Now" is a key attitude in counseling and therapy, and one may say the snags young Íñigo faced at this time were since he was unable to live in the "here and now." He was enthralled at the radiance of the feats he assumed he would embark upon after his conversion and concurrently upset at the disparity between what he now envisioned of himself and what he had been in the past. Being ensnared by his errors of the past, he sought to erase himself, but on doing so, however, his agitation increased, and he was gripped by anxiety. The basis of conversion is "Let go, let God." Regardless of what the situation may be, the mercy of God consists in believing that this world and the humans living here now are infused in all ways. I have dealt earlier with the importance of physicality. However, I wish to repeat here that unless we accept ourselves as embodied and living human beings, we have no choice but to run into agitation and disenchantment.

At that time however he steadily gained the ability to view himself objectively, as revealed by the words, "what new life is this we're beginning now?" [Au 21] What is interesting here is that his gradual regaining of himself, was done via the process of regaining his neglected human nature. A detailed route of recovery is not provided in the autobiography. What is stated is, "he began to mull over the means through which that spirit had come. As a result he decided, with great clarity, not to confess anything from the past any more." [Au 25] He carried out a switch between awareness and approach, what we now refer to as Cognitive Behavioral Therapy. Also, for the first time, he made a choice in favor of his body. "That led him to begin to doubt if these ideas were coming from the good spirit, and he came to the conclusion that it was better to leave them aside and to sleep for the allotted time; and so he did." [Au 26] This choice of his wherein he accepted his physicality, was indeed a major step. The *Autobiography* states, "the Lord willed that he woke up as if from sleep." [Au 25] This suggests that there was a spiritual transformation. It is reported that Íñigo began to accompany people, and when he came to find that rewarding, he stopped his various exaggerations, and began to care about his appearance. Even though it was a spiritual conversion, the body supported it. That is the reason why reasonable activities such as eating, sleeping, and relaxing, are vital.

In Manresa, he underwent the pain and fear of facing the darkness and evil that lurked within him, and he simultaneously experienced the hand of the merciful God that was stretched out towards him. Soon he would experience the illumination on the banks of the Cardoner River. His autobiography states, "the eyes of his understanding began to be opened ... and this with an enlightenment so strong that all things seemed new to him." [Au 30] He further says, "he received a great clarity in his understanding." [Au 30] In religious conversion, transformations occur not just in the regions of 'heart' and 'soul,' but also within 'reason' (psychologically we might also say 'cognition'). The two wheels of faith and reason are essential for good discernment. This became the vigor of Ignatian Spirituality, as well as its unique logic. Later it became the mainstay of the Spiritual Exercises, and in confronting darkness it plays the role of a thoughtful companion, so as to guide those who are confused by reason and emotion towards the light. The spirituality of Ignatius is a spirituality imbued with an understanding of the reality of human light and darkness.

A word about depression and desolation. Desolation according to Ignatius is not merely dejection or suffering. It is the work of the evil spirit. It is something that is triggered by spiritual causes. It is a trial conducted for the sake of spiritual maturity [Ex 7], or a means employed by the enemy to isolate human beings from God [Ex 317]. Depression and spiritual desolation can overlap, but it should be borne in mind that they differ. That is the reason why it is said that when in the state of heavy depression, one should refrain from the *Spiritual Exercises*. This is because not only would it not serve as a cure, there is on the contrary a danger of the issue being exacerbated. Nevertheless however, one can pray even in the state of depression. By prayer we can gain a great deal of consolation, and feel the support of God. In fact, in the case of mild depression, spiritual accompaniment can provide an effective occasion to open oneself to God. This is as viewed from the standpoint of Psycho-Spirituality.

In such a situation, people may behave in unstable ways due to the uncontrollable anger, anxiety, or loneliness that is aroused within them. We also, to varying degrees, experience some "depression," temporarily and in a range of ways. This could be because there exists a lack of balance between ideals and reality within ourselves, and our physicality has in consequence been neglected, or it might also perhaps arise because we have long remained in certain obscure feelings in the unconscious world around us. In a sense, the vicious circle that Íñigo had fallen into was also because he gave himself over to excessive temperance, without settling the disparity within him, between the reality existing and the ideals he pursued.

In Manresa, Íñigo encountered himself once again in the depths of his heart and experienced an unquenchable thirst for the things of this world. In this way, he gradually regained his physicality, as well as stability of heart and soul. Through the trials of the heart, his reason opened to the profound realms of his soul. At that time, having regained his composure, he began to walk. Since becoming a pilgrim implied having to walk, it had strong links to the recovery of his physicality. He began walking slowly along the path of his unique self-transcendence. The word Camino (road) is most appropriate for the experience of conversion. On the road, we at times get lost, and at times we detect new ways. We might say that Íñigo as a pilgrim was the authentic experience of Ignatian spirituality. It concerns walking, at times stopping, looking back, and continuing the search. It is an attitude of moving a step further (*Magis*), with a heart full of hope, without being satisfied with the status quo. After his Manresa experiences, on being free of his narcissistic attachments, Íñigo gained friends. What he desired more than anything else were fellow pilgrims, who would walk along with him. To maintain a balance between mind and body and obtain the joy of sharing, companions and communities are vital. His efforts in this regard finally bore fruit at the University of Paris after some cases of trial and error.

Once an incident has occurred, we cannot rewind the time and get back to it. Nevertheless, we can instead discover the power to live in it and gain fresh perceptions and insights, even though that may not be easy. Like Íñigo, we of the present time have also suffered some sorts of wounds or losses. Living with a wound means rediscovering the true value of one's hurt and buried self. In this world, even without our being aware of it, the ego gets inflated, and a fake self begins to walk alone. We may even call it an exaggerated delusion, but what enables a person to discover his true value is not the obduracy of saying, "it should be like this." Instead, it is in realizing one's ability to change and discovering one's motive and potential to live. One can become free of one's old self and "also become like this." Then one can be confident in one's new self. Íñigo faced a life wherein issues related to his bodily wound did not work out as planned. He was given a taste of human weakness and imperfection to the extent that he came to acquire a hatred for it.

Nevertheless, that was also when he realized his resilience, and it was a resilience promoted by God. His experience was one wherein he had reached rock bottom. However, God raised him, and he did not give up the idea of living once more.

On recalling the futility of being dominated by self-love and experiencing a thirst for God from the innermost recesses of his being, Íñigo's sensibilities and gaze sharpened, providing him with profundity and depth. His new self was full of awareness and gratitude at the fact of being alive. Íñigo communicated to others the profundity of this prayer that he had experienced. As he continued his journey, he shared this new spiritual sensitivity with others with whom he associated. While advancing onwards as a pilgrim, he became a contemplative who discovered God here and there and pursued his life of bonding with others. This nurtured within him a new, imaginative power and creativity, and so he acquired friends with whom he could share this way of life. It is indeed ironic, but without that cannonball blow, the Jesuits or Society of Jesus would not have been born. Thus, we see that living with wounds is painful, yet it provides us with the resilience to take that crucial step forward and foster the understanding of other people.

What does it mean to say, "seeing everything anew in Christ?" In Japan, where Christians constitute just about 2% of the entire population, the appeal to see things anew in Christ is not something that promptly comes to the fore within our minds. The same is true for students of Sophia University. Who is Christ? A personal encounter with him, dialogue with him, and other such issues that form the pivotal theme of spiritual life will not impact those who do not know Christ. Nevertheless, from his own conversion experience, Ignatius has bequeathed us a practical recommendation for spiritual life, namely to "find God in all things." That is the reason why a prior preliminary evangelization is necessary. If we were to observe the world through "new eyes," we would find it brimming with surprises that might be Christ. However, seeing with new eyes does not mean viewing things philosophically. Ignatius states, "he used to see with his interior eyes the humanity of Christ." [Au 29] In the course of his conversion, he was able to encounter the person of Christ. No one sees things from a height. There exists diversity among living people. Some people, at some point in their lives, suddenly notice issues, while others cannot grasp issues even though they constantly ponder over them. Ignatius also perhaps decided to pen an autobiography as he approached old age and came to relish life as he understood it. He was not a person who was holy and had a good grasp of things from the very start. Instead, he was obstinate and vacillated a lot. However, by encountering Christ and gradually cultivating a fresh outlook on life, and by being revitalized, accompanied, and desired by God, he was able to accept himself as an individual who was sent to the world as a storyteller of life.

Within Jesuit traditions, there is one tradition that guides human and spiritual voyages to the doorway of the 'surprise' of God. It is lengthy and slow, and takes considerable time. We Christians, and especially those of us who serve in the field of education, need to escort, interact, and share with the youth we deal with, on a daily basis. The 'surprise' referred to as Christ, is hidden within the mystery that is possessed by imperfect human beings. He is present within the sorrows of daily life, and in the midst of random unforeseen events, and he aids us in seeking out the presence of Christ within the light and shade of human nature, by drawing nearer to youthful 'Íñigos' of our current age. Now, due to the corona pandemic, more than ever before the need has arisen not just for mental care, but for care of the soul as well. I would like the young Íñigos to become pilgrims, to make friends, and walk along with them, so that they may proceed forward with confidence and hope. For that purpose, in the course of our human and spiritual wanderings, let us first trust in the power of God, and be aware that we are fellow pilgrims.

Let me finally end with the words of Fr. Nadal, who was familiar with Ignatius during his lifetime.

"Master Ignatius directed his attention to where the Holy Spirit and his vocation led him, and he followed the Holy Spirit with deep humility. He did not try to move ahead of the Holy Spirit. He entrusted his life to the unknown. This pilgrim was like a fool driven by his love for Jesus Christ. From the moment God entered his heart, he began traveling all over Europe in search of the best ways of love and service. His passion in life was to seek and find God in everything."

ホセ・ガルシア・デ・カストロ・ヴァルデス

1967 年スペイン・オビエド生まれ。1985 年イエズス会入会。1998 年司祭叙階。1999 年教皇庁立コミリャス大学で神学修士号取得。1999 年サラマンカ大学でスペイン文献学博士号取得。2001 年から教皇庁立コミリャス大学神学部教授。Colección Manresa の編集責任者（2007 年〜）。

著書に、*El Dios emergente: Sobre la consolación sin causa*, Bilbao 2001、*Diccionario de espiritualidad ignaciana* (ed.), Santander 2007、*Polanco: El Humanismo de los jesuitas (1517-1576)*, Madrid 2012、Ignacio de Loyola, *El Autógrafo de los Ejercicios espirituales* (ed.), Bilbao 2022 ほか多数。

酒井　陽介（さかい・ようすけ）

1971 年神奈川県生まれ。2001 年司祭叙階。2015 年イエズス会入会。2009 年教皇庁立グレゴリアン大学心理学科修士課程修了。2018 年教皇庁立グレゴリアン大学心理学科で心理学博士号取得。教皇庁立グレゴリアン大学心理学科講師（2020〜21 年）を経て、現在、上智大学神学部と同実践宗教学研究科で准教授として教鞭を執る。

著書に、*Self-transcendence in the Life of Pedro Arrupe, SJ. A Narrative Inquiry into His Writings*, Rome 2018 ほか。

川中　仁（かわなか・ひとし）

1962 年東京都生まれ。1984 年イエズス会入会。1995 年司祭叙階。1996 年上智大学神学研究科博士前期課程修了。2003 年ドイツ・ザンクトゲオルゲン哲学神学大学で神学博士号（Dr. theol.）取得。2004 年から上智大学で教鞭を執る。上智大学学生総務担当副学長（2014〜16 年）などを経て、現在、上智大学神学部教授、同神学部長（2017 年〜）、上智大学キリスト教文化研究所所長（2019 年〜）。

著書に、„*Comunicación". Die trinitarish-christozentrische Kommunikationsstruktur in den Geistlichen Übungen des Ignatius von Loyola*, Frankfurt a.M. 2005、イグナチオ・デ・ロヨラ『霊操』訳・解説、教文館、2023 年ほか。

José García de Castro Valdés, S.J.

He was born in Oviedo / Spain in 1967, entered the Society of Jesus in 1985, and was ordained a priest in 1998. In 1999 he completed the Master's program in Theology at the Pontifical Comillas University, and in 1999 he received a Doctorate in Hispanic Philology at Salamanca University. Since 2001 he has taught at the Pontifical Comillas University. He currently serves as professor of the university's Faculty of Theology, and Director of the *Colección Manresa* (from 2007).

His publications include, *El Dios emergente: Sobre la consolación sin causa*, Bilbao 2001; *Diccionario de espiritualidad ignaciana* (ed.), Santander 2007; *Polanco: El Humanismo de los jesuitas (1517-1576)*, Madrid 2012; IGNACIO DE LOYOLA, *El Autógrafo de los Ejercicios espirituales* (ed.), Bilbao 2022, and others.

Yosuke Sakai, S.J.

He was born in Kanagawa / Japan in 1971, was ordained a priest in 2001, and entered the Society of Jesus in 2015. In 2009 he completed the Master's program at the Institute of Psychology at Pontifical Gregorian University, and in 2018 he received a Doctorate in Psychology from the Pontifical Gregorian University in Rome. After teaching at the Institute of Psychology of the Pontifical Gregorian University (2020-2021), he currently serves as assistant professor of the Faculty of Theology and Graduate School of Applied Religious Studies, at Sophia University.

His publications include *Self-transcendence in the Life of Pedro Arrupe, SJ. A Narrative Inquiry into His Writings*, Rome 2018, and others.

Hitoshi Kawanaka, S.J.

He was born in Tokyo / Japan in 1962, entered the Society of Jesus in 1984, and was ordained a priest in 1995. In 1996 he completed the Master's program at the Graduate School of Theology at Sophia University, and in 2003 he received a Doctorate in Theology (Dr. Theol.) from the Sankt Georgen Graduate School of Philosophy and Theology in Germany. Since 2004 he has taught at Sophia University. After serving as Vice President for Student Affairs at Sophia University (2014-2016), he currently serves as professor, and Dean of the university's Faculty of Theology (from 2017), and Director of the university's Institute for Christian Culture (from 2019).

His publications include, *„Comunicación". Die trinitarish-christozentrische Kommunikations-struktur in den Geistlichen Übungen des Ignatius von Loyola*, Frankfurt a.M. 2005, and also a translation and commentary on Ignatius of Loyola's *Spiritual Exercises*, Tokyo 2023, and others.

キリストにおける新たなまなざし

2024年3月12日　第1版第1刷発行

編　者：川　　中　　　　　仁
発行者：ア ガ ス ティン　　サ リ
発　行：Sophia University Press
　　　　上　智　大　学　出　版

〒102-8554　東京都千代田区紀尾井町7-1
URL：https://www.sophia.ac.jp/

制作・発売　㈱ぎょうせい

〒136-8575　東京都江東区新木場1-18-11
URL：https://gyosei.jp
フリーコール　0120-953-431

〈検印省略〉

印刷・製本　ぎょうせいデジタル㈱
ISBN978-4-324-11372-1
（5300337-00-000）
［略号：（上智）新たなまなざし］

Sophia University Press

　上智大学は、その基本理念の一つとして、
「本学は、その特色を活かして、キリスト教とその文化を研
究する機会を提供する。これと同時に、思想の多様性を認
め、各種の思想の学問的研究を奨励する」と謳っている。

　大学は、この学問的成果を学術書として発表する「独自
の場」を保有することが望まれる。どのような学問的成果を
世に発信しうるかは、その大学の学問的水準・評価と深く
関わりを持つ。

　上智大学は、(1) 高度な水準にある学術書、(2) キリスト
教ヒューマニズムに関連する優れた作品、(3) 啓蒙的問題
提起の書、(4) 学問研究への導入となる特色ある教科書等、
個人の研究のみならず、共同の研究成果を刊行することに
よって、文化の創造に寄与し、大学の発展とその歴史に貢
献する。

Sophia University Press

One of the fundamental ideals of Sophia University is "to embody the university's special characteristics by offering opportunities to study Christianity and Christian culture. At the same time, recognizing the diversity of thought, the university encourages academic research on a wide variety of world views."

The Sophia University Press was established to provide an independent base for the publication of scholarly research. The publications of our press are a guide to the level of research at Sophia, and one of the factors in the public evaluation of our activities.

Sophia University Press publishes books that (1) meet high academic standards; (2) are related to our university's founding spirit of Christian humanism; (3) are on important issues of interest to a broad general public; and (4) textbooks and introductions to the various academic disciplines. We publish works by individual scholars as well as the results of collaborative research projects that contribute to general cultural development and the advancement of the university.

Seeing All Things New in Christ

© Ed. Hitoshi Kawanaka, 2024

published by
Sophia University Press

production & sales agency : GYOSEI Corporation, Tokyo
ISBN 978-4-324-11372-1
order : https://gyosei.jp